FIRELESS COOKERY

FIRELESS COOKERY

HEIDI KIRSCHNER

Madrona Publishers   *Seattle*   *1981*

FIRST EDITION

10 9 8 7 6 5 4 3 2 1

Published by
Madrona Publishers, Inc.
2116 Western Avenue
Seattle, Washington 98121

Drawings by the author.

Library of Congress Cataloguing in Publication Data

Kirschner, Heidi, 1913–
    Fireless cookery.

    Bibliography: p.
    Includes index.
    1. Fireless cookers.   I. Title.
TX831.K57   641.5'88   81-3772
ISBN 0-914842-58-7   AACR2

To the families of our world
for good cooking with less fuel

ACKNOWLEDGMENTS

Thanks to my mother for the idea and earliest experience with fireless cooking, and to my family who patiently ate what I cooked while I was learning. But thanks most of all to my husband, Franz, whose enthusiasm, criticism, wry jokes, and prodding encouraged me to start and to finish this book.

Contents

Introduction

Fireless cooking is an old and very useful method of food preparation that has been generally overlooked since World War II. The purpose of this book is to help revive it.

The fireless cooker works on the principle of keeping a container of food hot after a short initial cooking period on a heating unit. A fireless cooker may be any kind of enclosed container stuffed tightly with insulating material around a hollow space that is large enough to hold the average pot of soup or stew.

I grew up in Europe in a home with a variety of fireless cookers in daily use and have used one or more in my kitchen in the U.S. for more than forty years while raising a family and working as a pediatrician.

Whenever I expect family or friends for dinner I like to plan at least for one or two items on the menu to be cooked in the fireless cooker, not only for the sake of convenience and economy, but also for the extra dividend of pleasure when serving time comes. I enjoy watching everyone troop to the kitchen to be there when the cooker opens up like a magician's box. Those who know what to expect, particularly my grandchildren, bend over with expectant faces to sniff the aromas of good food, largely from our garden, and of warm hay from our meadow.

Friends who see the fireless cooker for the first time almost invariably respond with pleasure. Their remarks range from total surprise to fond childhood memories like, "My grandmother used to have a box just like it!" or "My mother used to tell us about a fireless cooker in her home in Europe." They all agree that the food is wonderful and that the old kitchen tool offers many conveniences, but no one remembers when or why it was abandoned and no one knows how to make or use one.

Over the decades I have shown many people how to build and use fireless cookers, but only in recent years have they become serious about using this kitchen tool regularly. Several forces have motivated this change in entrenched cooking habits: the energy crunch, a revived interest in old-fashioned, slowly cooked food, and the need for more and more cooks to be out of the home during the day.

It wasn't until my Hungarian husband and I came to North

America that I was forced to learn how fireless cookers are constructed. Franz could not help me, because he was studying ten or more hours a day for medical examinations, but he gave me a sheet of half-inch plywood for Christmas so I could make a cooker myself. I had made friends with our neighbors, and although no one quite understood what I was trying to do, they were all eager to assist me. I borrowed tools and was given leftover paint, but the best help came from the carpenter next door. He helped me figure out a workable pattern, taught me how to glue chunks of wood in strategic places to make the thing solid, and even gave me a tin can full of bent nails to straighten out, those being Depression days.

I started out bravely and got as far as the first few nails. That evening, however, I had a question to ask. I could hit a nail once or twice, I explained, but then I would hit almost anything else (including my thumb); wasn't there some good carpenter's trick he could show me? I can still see the smile spreading over his face. Of course he showed me once again, but he also told everybody in the neighborhood about the funny woman who wanted to learn how to hit a nail on the head. In the street or in the grocery store, people would stop to ask about my carpentry project and laugh and laugh. But it was a friendly laughter that got across a message: We know how you feel and we want to cheer you on. This little incident did a lot to help me feel accepted in our new country.

The cooker got done after a fashion, was promptly stuffed with

3

dried grass clippings from a vacant lot, and became a badly needed extra space to sit in our sparsely furnished apartment. I gradually learned how to use it and our older daughter, Ronnie, still uses it to cook for her family.

So, as a result of what I have learned, starting from that first inept carpentry project, I have written this book for friends and people everywhere who have requested instructions and recipes for a practical, ages-old method of food preparation: fireless cookery.

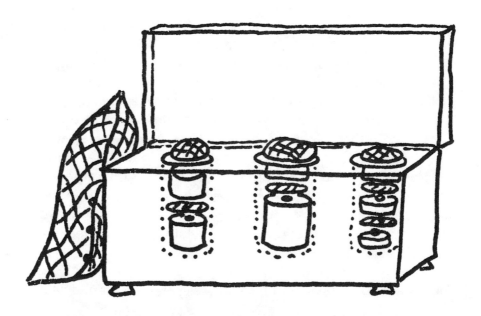

History and Advantages

Fireless cooking must be one of the oldest cooking systems in existence. It is simply a matter of bringing prepared food to a boil, lowering the heat to a simmer, placing the pot in a well-insulated container, and letting the cooking process finish with retained heat. Essentially, this is the same as cooking corn Indian-style in the embers of a campfire or cooking a Hawaiian luau in a mound of hot sand.

I learned about the fireless cooker during my childhood in Vienna, during World War I. In German the fireless cooker is called a *Kochkiste:* cooking box. There were ten people in our household—plus frequent guests—and since coal and wood were often unavailable and gas and electricity were rationed, the *Kochkiste* was important, if not essential.

Fireless cookers were also used on the farm where my family spent many summer vacations. There I heard a facetious story from the hired man about the invention of the fireless cooker.

One market day—went the tale—a farmer went to town to sell his produce. As soon as he was gone, his unfaithful wife invited her lover to share the stew she was cooking. But when the farmer came back unexpectedly, she hid the pot under the covers and the man under the bed. Hours later, after the farmer had finally returned to the market, the wife and her lover discovered that the stew was cooked to a turn.

Chances are, of course, that either the hired man or someone else made up the story, but I am sure this ancient kitchen tool must have been "invented" in similar ways many times over by farmers' wives who had good reason to hide their pots of precious food from strangers, uninvited neighbors, hostile governments, or conquering armies. Nothing would be more natural than to grab the pot already simmering on the stove and hide it in a bed, a chest of clothes, or a pile of hay—then, when the coast was clear, hours later, to discover that the stew was done!

Although use of this practical cooking method has diminished, it has by no means died out. The Swiss Army regularly uses fireless cookers to provide warm meals to mountain troops on maneuvers. Mules carry much of the heavy equipment—ammunition and artillery—and also haul the fireless cookers in special boxes. I have heard that there is a revival of the fireless cooker in England, particularly among older people. And in South Africa an organization called Women for Peace promotes the fireless cooker to help the native population, particularly in the countryside, maintain an inexpensive, nourishing diet and conserve scarce fuel. They sell the fireless cooker under the name Wonderbox together with a recipe booklet, *Wonder Cooking and Simply Living,* and promote the wonderbean—the soybean—because it is nutritionally excellent and can be grown easily and cooked in the fireless cooker.

In the United States, a cookbook published in 1909—*Mrs. Curtis's Cookbook*—devoted an entire chapter to fireless cookery. *Hints to Housewives,* published in 1917 in New York City by a municipal committee, details methods for fireless-cooker construction, suggesting asbestos or sawdust for insulation. *Joy of Cooking,* by Irma S. Rombauer and Marion Rombauer Becker, as recently as 1967 mentioned a fireless-cookery method. Willa Cather mentions a fireless cooker in *My Antonia,* a novel about midwestern rural life in the early part of the century.

ADVANTAGES OF THE FIRELESS COOKER

Obviously, the fireless cooker's time has come again. We are all becoming conscious of the need to conserve energy, and of the sharply rising price of electricity and other fuels—to double or more in the near future.

However, I would like to convince my fellow cooks that unlike some plans to save energy, the fireless cooker is not cumbersome, boring, or time-consuming, but exactly the opposite. It's time-saving and fun! It also offers many other advantages:

It produces particularly tasty and attractive food that retains its shape and color.

Energy consumption is reduced by three to twenty times.

It simplifies meal preparation because one or more items on the menu can be made ahead of time, put in the cooker, and left without supervision until serving.

Many very good recipes abandoned because they take too long can be returned to our tables because cooking and supervision time are considerably shortened.

Failures are rare. Food is very unlikely to stick or burn because the simmering time is short and supervised, and nothing can burn once it's in the cooker. Overcooking is impossible—after the brief stove-top boiling stops, the temperature decreases in a gradual, controlled way, so food gets done but does not disintegrate.

Food doesn't boil over onto the stove, causing clean-up problems later on, because the cook is always present for the short simmering time.

Money can be saved at the butcher shop because inexpensive cuts of meat become tender with this cooking method.

In summer the kitchen stays cool.

The fireless cooker is safe for children: my own many years ago, my grandchildren today, and everyone else's.

Nutrients are, by and large, better preserved than with other cooking methods because the boiling point is maintained only briefly; after that the gradually decreasing temperature processes foods gently, without destroying the nutrients.

Timing is very flexible once the pot is in the cooker. Food can be kept warm without risk of overcooking, and with no need to reheat for latecomers.

A portable fireless cooker is ideal for picnicking, camping, or boating (see the section on Other Uses).

The fireless cooker makes entertaining easy. Food preparation is complete, except for last-minute touches, two or three hours before dinnertime.

Fireless cooking solves the problem of cooking for large groups—twenty to thirty people. I have often improvised a fireless cooker for such occasions by lining our attractive

Chinese weed basket, which measures 18 inches high by 20 inches across, with newspaper, stuffing it like any other cooker, and placing a pillow on top. This accommodates my spaghetti kettle, which is 8 inches tall by 10 inches across, and holds 10 quarts. Then I simply double or triple my usual recipes for soups, stews, or one-dish dinners. We particularly enjoy watching our guests arrive, sniff and look around surprised to see no preparations for dinner until the youngest child points to the old weed basket in the middle of the living room. Everyone laughs as the pillow comes off. Helpings are ladled out, then lid and pillow are promptly put back on to keep the food hot for second helpings.

One final point, and perhaps the most significant of all, is the intangible advantage of the fireless cooker. The type of food that lends itself best to this method is usually easy to stretch to accommodate unexpected guests. My husband and I value the easy sharing and informal hospitality our family can provide —in part, at least, because of the fireless cooker.

THE FIRELESS COOKER VERSUS THE CROCKPOT

While the crockpot, using low-temperature cooking for prolonged periods, shares some advantages with the fireless cooker, it is not as useful for the following reasons:

Fireless cooking uses less fuel.

The fireless cooker can be left unattended with no concerns about electrical hazards.

The fireless cooker is less expensive.

Cooking times generally are shorter in the fireless cooker than in the crockpot.

Foods in the crockpot inevitably are overcooked after 8 or 10 hours of continued heat, no matter how low. In contrast, food in the fireless cooker cannot overcook because the heat is gradually decreasing.

Note, however, that many of the recipes given for crockpots can be easily adapted to the fireless cooker.

THE FIRELESS COOKER VERSUS THE PRESSURE COOKER

The pressure cooker, while offering a method of saving the cook's time, cooks foods under high pressure—a system that results in foods of inferior taste and appearance. However, a pressure cooker makes an excellent pot for use inside the fireless cooker because of its tight lid.

Making or Buying a Cooker

SUITABLE MATERIALS AND READY-MADE CONTAINERS

A fireless cooker can be made from several types of material or from various kinds of containers. What you use will depend partly on where you want to store the cooker and whether it's to double as a piece of furniture. Some of the materials or containers I've used are:

> A corrugated cardboard box. If you're trying out fireless cookery and want to begin with an inexpensive, easy-to-make, one-pot cooker, this is what I would recommend. Lightweight and easy to store, with protective paint, varnish, or adhesive paper, it will last you several years.

> A wooden box. For a single pot, another easy and inexpensive fireless cooker can be constructed of quarter-inch plywood with wooden braces at the corners. If you're thinking in terms of a cooker that will serve as a low table or seat, you'll need sturdier wood and you might want to consider legs. If you could use a high kitchen stool, I recommend a tall cooker that accommodates two pots, stacked, and is high enough to sit on while doing kitchen chores—about 24 inches high. In this case the pots will be separated by a fat round pillow, so that the top pot can be taken out while the bottom one remains undisturbed.

> A deep drawer (12 inches high or more), if not too far away from the stove.

A basket large enough to hold the stuffing. No lid is necessary if the pillow on top is 6 to 7 inches thick.

Canvas, denim, or any other reasonably sturdy fabric. In this case you'll be making a portable cooker, and you'll want to make a tough drawstring closure and handles.

DIMENSIONS OF A FIRELESS COOKER

The dimensions of a fireless cooker will vary, depending on your needs and your storage situation. The only basic rule is that your container be at least 4 inches larger in each direction (top,

MAKING MY FIRST FIRELESS COOKER

bottom, and sides) than your most frequently used pot. Larger pots, like a 4- or 6-quart kettle, can be squeezed in, and smaller pots are accommodated when the stuffing is rearranged closely around them.

It's best to use a casserole-type pot with a small handle on each side; if you're using a saucepan with a single handle, you'll have to allow space for the handle. If the handle is more than 3 inches long, you may have trouble tucking it in.

If you want to accommodate several pots, a footlocker, oblong trunk, or window seat will hold two or more nests and each nest can hold two or three pots.

If your cooker is to double as a seat, I recommend the type my mother used. It was about 18 inches high, was wide enough for sitting comfort (also about 18 inches), and was long enough for two or three people to sit on at once. It held three nests of various sizes, each nest accommodating one to three pots separated by pillows. It was constructed of solid lumber, furnished with handles at each end and legs, and painted for easy cleaning.

If your container is quite large, as a window seat might be, the extra space can simply be filled with whatever you're using to stuff the cooker, or seldom-used blankets or pillows can be stored at one end. It is important, however, that all extra space be full to avoid large air pockets, which would interfere with the efficiency of the cooker.

STUFFING

Any materials on hand in your home that are usable for packing fragile objects or for stuffing pillows or soft toys can also be used for stuffing a fireless cooker. The basic criterion is that the stuffing fill all the space around the pot, so a soft material—for example, polyester fiberfill—works best.

Hay or straw works well. Probably the oldest stuffings for the fireless cooker, they're nice for traditionalists!

Lawn clippings will work—if thoroughly dried.

Excelsior or shredded newspaper is excellent.

Feather or dacron pillows are fine for the top.

Sawdust or wood shavings can be used, but only in pillowcases—otherwise they are messy.

Polystyrene pellets (the kind used for beanbag furniture) are widely available at stores where yard goods are retailed, and in my opinion are the best stuffing available. Their insulating qualities are superior, they adapt particularly well to the size and shape of different pots, and they can be readily washed in case there is a spill. (But they must be line dried because an automatic dryer may melt them.) Their static electricity makes the pellets hard to handle, however. When you put them into a pillow, stuff them loosely, and sew the pillow securely. *Pillows stuffed with polystyrene pellets drape so well that only a top and bottom pillow are needed*—your cooker won't need a middle one.

Polyester fiberfill also gets my highest recommendation.

Foam rubber pillows are handy particularly to cover the bottom or the top of a cooker. For a while I used a cooker made of several layers of foam rubber with holes cut in the middle for my pots. But I abandoned this method because it is less flexible than other methods: the foam rubber has no give, and I ended up with a cooker that fit only one size pot.

Shredded foam rubber encased in pillow slips can be used if you have it on hand, but I don't recommend it otherwise —it's difficult to work with because of its static electricity, and very messy.

DECORATION AND FINISH

I think that a fireless cooker, like any other kitchen tool, should be attractive as well as practical. For the outside, paint, varnish, or any finish that allows washing or wiping is suitable.

For the inside, I drape a cloth over the hay or dacron, or I make a pillowcase to enclose the polystyrene pellets or sawdust. Sometimes I use patchwork—it's attractive and doesn't cost a cent.

COMMERCIALLY BUILT FIRELESS COOKERS

In the past, many types of fireless cookers were produced and marketed under various trade names. One, with a metal lining, was made in about 1900 and is on display in a museum in Bellingham, Washington. Others are advertised in old

CONSTRUCTION OF CARDBOARD FIRELESS COOKER

Cooker dimensions: 18″ x 18″ x 18″

Materials and tools
Corrugated cardboard sheets, which are sold for a moderate price by paper boxboard manufacturers (listed in Yellow Pages of telephone book)
Pencil
Yardstick
Razor-type cutting knife
Paper glue

Cut the two basic pieces, one 68″ x 24¼″ and the other 23″ x 23″. Using a pencil or the dull edge of a table knife, score the two pieces along the dotted lines indicated in the diagrams. Cut notches in the square piece as shown to make corner flaps for the lid. Make the lid by bending in the cardboard along the scored lines (using the side of a table to assure even bending) and glue corner flaps in place. Make the box by bending the bottom flaps of opposite sides so they meet in the middle, forming a double bottom, and glue. Bend and glue the side flap to the inside of the side edge.

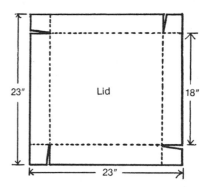

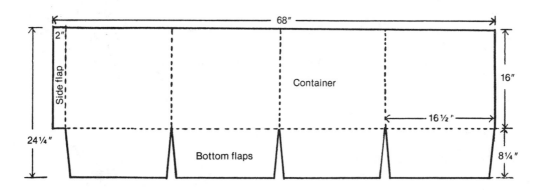

CONSTRUCTION OF PLYWOOD FIRELESS COOKER

Cooker dimensions: 18″ x 18″ x 18″

Materials
Wood glue and 4-penny nails for attaching all wooden parts
Two 2″ loose-pin hinges (optional)

Bottom
> 1 piece ½″ plywood 17½″ x 17½″
> 4 pieces 1″ plywood 3″ x 3″ for optional legs

Sides
> 4 pieces ¼″ plywood 16″ x 17¾″
> 4 pieces ¼″ plywood 17½″ x 3″ for lip on inside upper edge

Top
> 1 piece ¼″ plywood 18″ x 18″

Braces
> 4 pieces 1″ x 1″ stock 15″ long for bottom
> 4 pieces 1″ x 1″ stock 11″ long for side corners
> 4 pieces 1″ x 1″ stock 17½″ long for inside lid

Construction (glue and nail *all* joinings)
1. Attach 15″ braces to bottom board, flush with board edges, leaving a 1″ open square at each corner. Side braces will fit into those corners.
   Attach a long edge of each side piece (17¾″) to the sides of the bottom. Sides meet side to end at corners; each piece has one raw end showing, one covered. Attach sides to each other.
2. Attach top to form a closed cube. Saw the cube 2½″ below the top (step 2). (Or, for a small fee, get a lumber store to do it for you.) The top piece is the lid.
3. Attach the side corner braces, fitting them into the space left for them on the bottom. They will not reach to the top of the sides because space has been left to make a lip (step 3).
4. Make a lip by attaching the 3″ x 17½″ pieces to the inside of the upper edge of the box, allowing them to protrude ½″ above the top of the box. Attach the remaining braces to the inside of the lid.
5. Add—if you want to—legs and hinges. Legs should be attached to the bottom board, not the bottom and sides. Hinges for the lid should be attached with nuts and bolts (screws pull out).

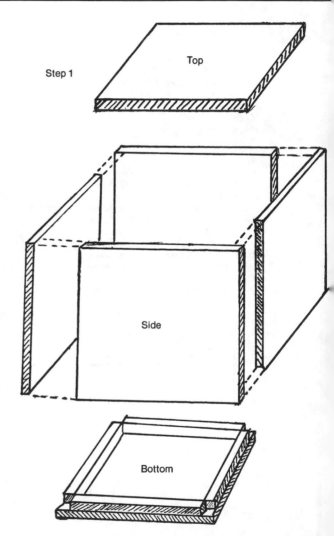

Step 1 · Top · Side · Bottom

Step 2

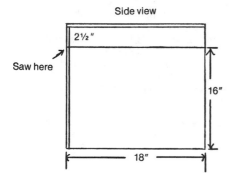

Side view

2½"

Saw here

16"

18"

Step 3

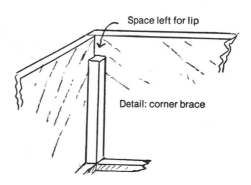

Space left for lip

Detail: corner brace

Step 4

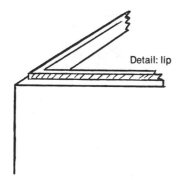

Detail: lip

Step 5

Bottom view showing legs.
Note arrangement of side pieces.

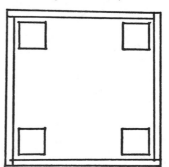

Step 1

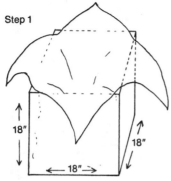

18″

18″

18″

Step 2

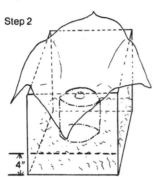

4″

STUFFING A ONE-POT FIRELESS COOKER

Cooker dimensions: 18″ x 18″ x 18″

1. Drape a 40″ x 40″ square of fabric in the cooker, with the corners of the fabric folded over the sides of the cooker (step 1).
2. Cover the bottom of the fabric with an insulating material at least 4″ deep and place a pot in the center (step 2).
3. Pack more insulating material tightly around the pot, then remove the pot, leaving a nest.
4. Turn the corners of the fabric inward, lining the nest and enclosing all the insulating material (step 4).
5. Hem a 32″ x 32″ square of cheerful cotton fabric, fit it inside the nest, and tuck in the corners along the cooker walls for a washable cover that helps keep the insulation in place (step 5).

For a two-nester follow the same procedure as above for each nest. Then place the nests side by side in a larger box. A wooden or cardboard partition between nests is not essential but makes the job easier.

Step 3

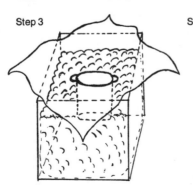

Step 4

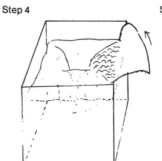

Step 5

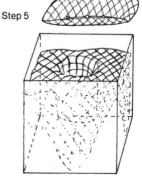

20

REMOVABLE PILLOWS FOR A FIRELESS COOKER

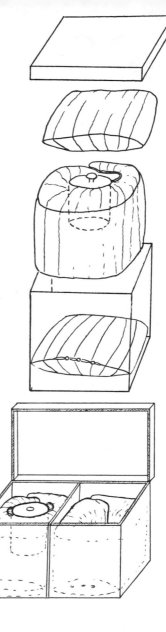

Cooker dimensions: 18" x 18" x 18"

1. Make a pillow for the top of the container and a pillow for the bottom. Prior to stitching, the squares for the pillows will measure 21" x 21". Stitch on sides, with a 1" seam allowance.
2. Stuff with foam rubber chips, sawdust, or whatever, and stitch on the fourth side.
3. Make a long pillow to wrap around the pot: dimensions of each pillow piece prior to stitching will be 13" x 80"; 1" seam allowance. Stuff the pillow.
4. Make a removable cover for all three pillows, using washable fabric.
5. Before using a cooker stuffed in this method, set up the bottom pillow and the long pillow in the container (ends of the long pillow overlapping) to make sure the pot fits. Adjust overlap to accommodate pots of different sizes.
6. For a cooker of different dimensions, plan the top and bottom pillows to be the same dimensions as cooker lid and bottom plus 3". For the long pillow, plan on the pre-sewing width to be container height minus 5", and the presewing length to be container girth plus 8".
7. Use this method for any number of adjoining nests (top pillows not shown in drawing of two-nester).
   Note: If your pillow stuffing is polystyrene pellets, there is no need for the middle pillow because the pellets in top and bottom pillows conform so completely to the shape of the pot.

MAKING A PORTABLE FIRELESS COOKER
(Sufficient for a 2-quart pot)

Materials
2⅓ yards of denim or similar sturdy material 36″ wide

2⅔ yards of cord for drawstrings (3-ply cotton or similar nylon cord)

Enough corrugated cardboard to make a rectangle 10″ x 44″ (to curve inside the portable cooker so sides will stand up), and a 12¼″ circle to give strength to the bottom. Not necessary with foam-rubber lining.

Stuffing. Any kind works; here I've used newspaper because it's easily obtainable, inexpensive, and neat.

Making the cooker
1. Cut the denim. The main piece will be 36″ wide and 42″ long. Cut 2 strips 36″ long and 5″ wide; 2 circles 18″ in diameter; and 2 circles 13″ in diameter.
2. The 2 strips will be handles. For each handle, fold the sides inward, one edge overlapping the other. Fold the top edge so it has a narrow hem. Stitch. You should have a handle about 2″ wide. For added strength, stitch along the sides as well. Attach to the sides of the bag at slight angles about 4″ from what will be the bag bottom and 4″ from what will be the sides (indicated in step 1). Make a narrow hem on both sides of the 25″ slit in the bag, and make a hem the same length on the two edges parallel to the slit.

3. Fold the material in half on the dotted lines indicated in step 1. An inch from the fold, pin and then make a row of stitching; parallel to this, about 1″ away, make another row of stitching to form a tunnel for the cord (step 3).

With the right sides together, pin, baste, and stitch the bottom of the portable cooker (the 42″ length) to a 13″ circle. Allow a ¾″ seam allowance for the bag's side seam, which has not yet been stitched.

Stitch the side seam up to point X where the narrow hem ends (step 3). You now have, in effect, a bag with a round bottom and two loose flaps that will serve as a lining.

4. If your insulation is soft—it will be unless you use foam rubber sheets—line the sides of the cooker with the rectangle of cardboard, stapled together at the ends, and lay the cardboard circle on the bottom. The lining flaps fold in to cover the insulation on the sides. On each side, run a short cord through the eyelets (step 4) to hold the lining in place (just above the cardboard). Eyelets are indicated by 8 small circles in step 1.

Cut the drawstring cording in half and run the cords through the tunnel in opposite directions to make drawstrings. Knot the ends together on each side.

Step 1

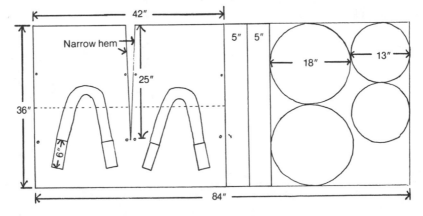

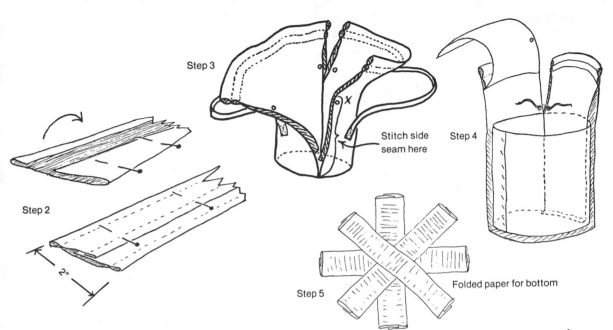

Step 2

Step 3

2"

Stitch side seam here

Step 4

Step 5

Folded paper for bottom

Folded papers overlapping for sides

Stuffing the cooker

5. Turn the lining out, exposing the cardboard. Take 7 layers of an open newspaper and fold them into thirds lengthwise, making a strip about 7" x 27". Make several such strips (you'll need 1 or 2 Sunday papers for the total job) and lay 3 strips across the bottom of the bag; the centers will intersect and they'll look like an asterisk, as in step 5. To line the sides, place two strips, long sides down and ends overlapping, to make one circle against the cardboard.

Make another asterisk and, above that, one more side layer. (As the bottom is built up, the sides will get higher.)

Continue to add newspaper strips on the bottom and sides until you have insulation about 3" thick.

Fold in the lining, which will hold the papers in. Hem the second 13" circle to cover the bottom.

Make a pillow for the top from the 18" circles and stuff them with shredded newspaper. Make a washable pillowcase to cover.

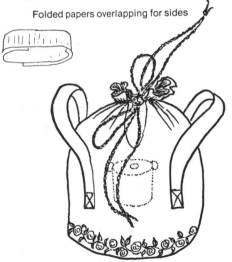

23

IDEAS WANTED

Aprovecho Institute, a nonprofit organization in Eugene, Oregon, is developing information on fireless cookers in order to disseminate fuel-conserving ideas to the Third World. Members of the group have built several models of fireless cookers—which they refer to as the Haybox Cooker—that are now being tested. Tried so far: aluminum-foil-wrapped cardboard boxes, styrofoam-filled pillows, and rigid-foam building insulation. To be tested: a wide range of natural materials for stuffing, including feathers, coconut hulls, rice hulls, raw cotton, scraps of cloth, peanut hulls, and sawdust. Aprovecho's goal is to develop low-cost models that can be built anywhere in the world with locally available materials.

Aprovecho would like to exchange information with people who know about indigenous methods of cooking with retained heat. Write to Margaret Thomas, Aprovecho Institute, 442 Monroe Street, Eugene, OR 97402. Besides Aprovecho, there's me! I would be delighted to hear about new ideas. Address me in care of Madrona Publishers, 2116 Western Avenue, Seattle, WA 98121.

cookbooks; *Mrs. Curtis's Cookbook* carries an ad for the United States Fireless Cooker. *Joy of Cooking*, 1967 edition, mentions a commercial cooker that uses a brick heated in the oven and placed in the bottom of the cooker to help retain heat, a system that seems cumbersome and inferior to the homemade fireless cooker.

A great improvement over commercially produced fireless cookers of the past is the Meal Minder, a commercially built cooker recently made available in the United States. It's washable, attractive, and lightweight (less than two pounds); I've tested it myself, and I like it. For information on the Meal Minder, write Sheila's Kitchen, Inc., P.O. Box 267, Sea Cliff, New York 11579.

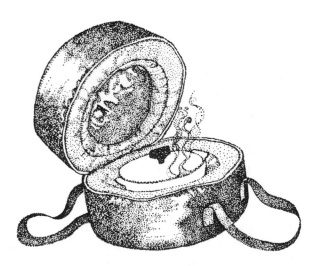

Learning to Use the Cooker

WHERE TO PUT IT

If you have a large kitchen, for instance the kind with a family-size breakfast area in it, there should be no problem finding a place for your fireless cooker. A standard one-nest cooker will easily fit under the table, under a chair, or on the lower shelf of a table. In our cabin we have a large wooden fireless cooker that doubles as a seat for one or two people and fits under a window. But in the small kitchen we have in town, it becomes difficult to find a good spot. We solved the problem by using two deep drawers 12 inches high and 16 by 20 inches at the base. They are located right next to the stove, which is ideal. But any drawer of the right size will do *if* it's in the kitchen. If it's in another room, too much heat is lost in transport. If there are no appropriate drawers, there is sometimes space under the sink or in a broom closet. Sometimes a shelf can be removed from a low cupboard to give enough height. If space can be found in the kitchen, it will still be necessary to take the box out of its storage place and put it next to the stove at preparation time so that the pot can be placed in the cooker promptly and the lid closed. It is best if the fireless cooker can stay there until serving time, but if you have to move it out of the way, be sure to keep it level!

When not in use, cookers can be stored wherever there is room. If they're made of cardboard they don't weigh much and can easily be stored in a closet, on a high shelf, or on top of the refrigerator.

If you want more than one cooker you may have to look for imaginative solutions. For everyday cooking, including dinner parties for six to eight people, I feel adequately equipped with the nests in my two drawers, each of which holds a pot of up to 6-quart capacity, but if I plan a larger party I stuff insulation into

our round garden basket (18 inches high by 20 inches across) and cover it with a 7-inch-thick pillow.

A portable cooker is nice to have, particularly as a second cooker. It will be in use less often than your main cooker so there's no reason why it can't be stored some distance from the kitchen. Made of reasonably sturdy, colorful cotton, a portable fireless cooker would make a pretty ornament hanging from a hook somewhere in the kitchen. So if you cook in a mini-kitchen, an attractive portable cooker hanging from the door-knob of a cupboard may be the answer for your first fireless cooker.

THE RIGHT POTS

Use only pots with tight-fitting lids. *This is very important.* Rubber bands stretched over the lid and handles of a pot are a good makeshift method of assuring a tight fit.

Since the process starts out on a conventional stove-top heating unit, use only pots that can tolerate direct heat.

Choose a pot of a size that allows the food to fill it about two-thirds full or to within 2 inches of the top. This "head room" is necessary to allow space for building up steam. If there is less space on top, the steam will lift the lid and the pot may boil over. The heat and steam needed for fireless cooking will escape. But the pot should not be too large for the amount of food

you intend to cook. If there is a small amount of food in the bottom of a big pot, and a lot of head room above, heat and steam will dissipate too quickly. The pots should be of average proportions, neither tall and narrow nor wide and shallow.

Pay attention to the length of the handles on your pots if you're not using two-handled casseroles. Short handles (3 inches or less) will work; long handles will not work, because a snug tuck-in is not possible.

The materials your pots are made of will vary. From my own experience I can tell you that a cast-iron Dutch oven with an appropriate lid is usually excellent. Aluminum is fine. Aluminum camping utensils often have convenient folding handles and work very well—in fact, they resemble pots made specifically for fireless cookers used in Europe in the past. Stainless steel pots with tight-fitting sleeve-type lids are also excellent.

Ceramic pots are fine if they can tolerate direct heat for the simmering period and if they have tight lids—which many of them don't.

A pressure cooker, used simply as a pot, is fine because of its reliable, tight-fitting lid. Simply do the simmering with the pressure cooker weight *off*, then place the pot in the fireless cooker and put the weight on after the pot is nested, just before you cover the pot with the pillow.

My own "family" of pots are of heavy, enameled cast-iron with heavy lids. The biggest is a 6-quart casserole. The next largest holds 4 quarts and is used mostly for larger quantities of potatoes or soup. My most frequently used pot—3½ quarts—is for stews, and soups when there are fewer people to feed. My 2-quart pot, which I consider the smallest practical size for use in a fireless cooker, is handy for smaller amounts of rice or other grains and for cooking root vegetables like beets or turnips.

I supplement these pots with a 10-quart aluminum spaghetti-and-canning kettle when I'm having a large party, and, at the other extreme, once in a while I put my 3-cup short-handled saucepan into the cooker with a dab of sauce or vegetables—but only for an hour or less and only to keep something warm.

TIMING

The first step for preparing your fireless-cooker meal is the same as for any meal: cut, slice, chop, or otherwise prepare the foods. Combine all the ingredients, and, bearing in mind the importance of using a pot of the right size, bring them to a boil over your usual heating unit, then reduce to a simmer.

Simmering time starts when you cover the pot and reduce the heat to simmer. This must be timed accurately. Otherwise, food will be disappointing: underdone, overdone, stuck to the pot, or simply not as attractive as it ought to be. I would advise (from hard-learned experience) that while food is simmering you clean up the dishes or kitchen, rather than going away, perhaps being distracted, and losing track of time. Don't peek inside the pot —you'll throw off the timing.

NO PEEKING !

Have your cooker right next to the stove. As soon as the simmering time is over, use two potholders, hold your pot on both sides with your thumbs firmly on the lid so that no steam escapes, put the pot promptly into the fireless cooker, tuck the pillow tightly around it, and close the fireless cooker.

Cooker time is the period your food spends in the fireless cooker. Cooker time is flexible! The cooker times given for each recipe are minimum cooker times. This means that at any time after that, up to several hours later, the food will be done to a turn: not overdone, but hot and ready to serve.

RECIPES TO START WITH

A cook who starts to think about dinner only when she or he gets hungry may think it's too late that day to use the cooker. But many recipes in this book require only 1 to 5 minutes' simmering time and only 1 hour's cooker time, and several others require little more.

Even for those who have no trouble planning ahead, I think the best way to start is with a basic food with a short cooker time, such as rice or potatoes, doing the rest of your dinner in the conventional manner.

After you are confident that your cooker is well stuffed, all heat leaks are eliminated, and you are using the right pot for the amount of food you are preparing, gradually try recipes with longer cooker periods. A one-pot dinner, soup, or stew is the most rewarding. But until you gather some experience, I would like to suggest that you allow about one quarter-hour before serving time for taking your dinner out of the cooker to check if all is well so you will still have time to fix it if something is amiss (see Trouble Shooting).

THE BEST FOODS FOR THE FIRELESS COOKER

Foods that require long cooking periods are the best candidates for the fireless cooker. The fireless cooker is most helpful for the more inexpensive cuts of meat (like stew meat and pot roast) or for root vegetables (like beets and potatoes), grains (barley or the old-fashioned long-cooking oats and rice), or long-cooking beans. It is pointless to cook spaghetti in the fireless cooker; pasta takes only 5 to 10 minutes anyway, should be kept *al dente*, and would only get mushy in the cooker. The same is true of most fruit, which gets too soft if cooked more than 2 or 3 minutes. Friends of mine, however, tell me they like to cook

rhubarb in the fireless cooker because it produces a particularly lovely red color and good flavor.

QUANTITIES

Not too little. Little dabs of food in small saucepans don't work
because heat and steam dissipate too quickly. If your family is
small, plan to cook a dish that can be used for two or three
meals.

Not too much. Generally, anything larger than a 6-quart kettle in
a fireless cooker is unmanageable. Use two pots instead! (True,
in a few selected recipes I have suggested amounts that will take
a 10-quart kettle—but usually these are for improvised cookers,
definitely not for frequent use.) Always keep in mind the rule of
thumb: the food in the fireless cooker should fill about two-
thirds of the pot or be about 2 inches from the top.

HOW TO ADAPT RECIPES TO FIRELESS COOKING

Choose recipes that lend themselves to fireless cooking.

Good candidates are:

> Soups; stews; meats that require long cooking periods; dried beans, dried peas, or lentils; and large root vegetables such as potatoes, onions, or carrots.
>
> Recipes like the ones your grandmother used to make.
>
> Grains in combination with vegetables.
>
> Recipes requiring steaming.

Poor candidates are:

> Foods that require only very short cooking periods (spinach or fresh fruit, for example).
>
> Foods that cannot or should not be cooked in large amounts of liquid—as in cases where the liquids are discarded, taking many of the nutrients with them.
>
> Foods that become unattractive when cooked slowly (fresh greens or green peas).

Suppose your old stew recipe reads, roughly, "Cut up and fry ½ pound salt pork and sauté onion, garlic, and herbs in the pork drippings. Brown in this mixture 2 pounds of beef cut up for stew, add liquid, simmer for 2 to 3 hours. For the last hour of cooking, add 4 tablespoons sherry; 15 minutes before serving add carrots and potatoes cut into 1-inch pieces. Thicken, season, and garnish with chopped parsley."

The entire recipe can be followed as it is, up to the point where it says "simmer for 2 to 3 hours." At this point you start the simmering time given for fireless-cooker stew: about 20 to 30 minutes. Place your stew in the fireless cooker and expect the cooker time to be close to one and a half times the suggested cooking time given in your old recipe. The 2 to 3 hours would be 3 to 4½ hours. You may want to experiment with shortening that cooker time until you know what your minimum cooker time is for this particular stew. At the point where your old recipe says, "For the last hour of cooking, add 4 tablespoons sherry; 15 minutes before serving add carrots and potatoes," I would suggest: 1 hour before serving, add the vegetables and sherry, bring to a boil, cover, simmer 5 minutes, and return to the cooker.

Another example. You have a good recipe for pot roast. Proceed with the recipe until you get to the point where it says, "cover and bake for 2 hours or more." At this point *check to see that there is enough liquid* to fill your pot two-thirds full or about 2 inches from the top. Add broth or other liquid as necessary, make certain it boils, cover, reduce heat, simmer 20 to 30 minutes, and place the pot in the fireless cooker. Cooker time will be close to one and a half times the oven time suggested in the old recipe.

If you have been successful several times in adapting a recipe, experiment with shortening the cooker time gradually to establish minimum cooker time. If your adaptations have not been successful, consult the chapter on Trouble Shooting.

You may find that you want to use your fireless cooker for a single element of a conventional recipe. For instance, there are many recipes where the most important aspect is a fancy sauce. The sauce is often too involved to do in the last half-hour before serving, so simplify life by making it ahead of time and putting it in the cooker. With many fish soups, only the sauce or the liquid requires a long cooking period; the fish or seafood is added only for the last 10 or 15 minutes. Make the sauce or soup ahead of time in your fireless cooker, and add your fish just before serving. Or top off a briefly sautéed fish with a sauce made in the cooker.

FOOD SAFETY

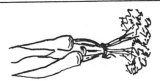

It is always important to use special care when cooking meat, poultry, or fish. If any of these have been frozen, make sure they are completely thawed before cooking. The United States Department of Public Health has determined the temperature of safety against ordinary household food contamination to be 145°F. Cooking with retained heat in a fireless cooker means that the food cooks while the temperature drops very slowly. I have checked innumerable times, using many different amounts and types of foods and sizes of pots, and found that for up to 4 hours — and often much longer — food stays steaming hot in the cooker, and the temperature is at or above 145°F. If you have a thermometer, check for your own satisfaction. Should you want to leave the food in the cooker for longer periods for convenience, or if you suspect that the food may have cooled off, just bring it back to the boiling point and simmer it for 5 minutes to be absolutely sure it won't spoil.

Food left in the cooker for more than twenty-four hours should be discarded.

Recipes

The recipes that follow were selected with two considerations in mind: to give the cook an opportunity to gain experience with this method by using the staples of a daily menu, and to offer as many types of recipes as possible, requiring various kinds of preparation, from boiling to steaming to yoghurt-making.

Quite a few recipes were selected because they are our family favorites; with these I have the most experience to share. Others were added with traditional American cooking in mind, to help people learn to use a new kitchen tool while cooking familiar foods. Still others were included in the hope that my fellow cooks, having saved so much time and effort through use of the fireless cooker, will be inspired to move onward to new cooking adventures.

Soups and Stock

All soup recipes here are planned for a 3½-quart pot, and will be ample to feed 6 people. I like to make soup in quantity in order to have it on hand for a few days, and also because it freezes well. Use about half the amounts suggested here if you want to use a 2-quart pot, but be sure to have the pot about two-thirds full—filled to about 2 inches from the top.

Stock is the flavorful, nutritional broth extracted from meat or fish by simmering. It may be served plain as a thin, clear soup, or it can be the base from which a variety of sauces, stews, aspics, and several other dishes are made. The outer leaves of cabbage and other greens, and any end-of-the-season vegetables considered too tough or too strong in taste, bruised or stringy celery tops and outside stalks, parsley roots, and many other vegetables or vegetable parts are excellent additions to the stock pot. So are many trimmings and leftover meat, poultry, fish, and liquids in which vegetables, dumplings, or meat have been boiled.

Beef Stock

SIMMERING TIME: 15 MINUTES
COOKER TIME: 3 TO 4 HOURS

2 pounds beef shank or marrow bones, cut into 2-inch
    sections
2 teaspoons salt
4 quarts cold water
2 pounds beef trimmings, or other inexpensive cuts
1 large onion, unpeeled
1 large carrot
1 leek, tops trimmed to leave 2 to 3 inches of green
1 turnip
1 green, outside stalk celery or ½ celeriac (celery root),
    when in season
½ bay leaf
6 peppercorns
1 bouquet garni, consisting of 3 sprigs parsley, 3 sprigs
    thyme, and 1 sprig rosemary, tied together with string
4 cloves garlic, peeled

In 6-quart pot, combine beef shank, salt, and cold water. Bring
to boil and skim with slotted spoon. Add all other ingredients,
return to boiling, and skim again. Cover, reduce heat, simmer
for 15 minutes, and place in cooker for 3 to 4 hours. Strain, reserving meat for use with hash or, if tender enough, for meat
salad. Reserve attractive vegetables to dice and serve with vege-

table soup, and discard the rest. Refrigerate broth long enough to allow fat to rise to top for easy removal, about 30 minutes, then store in refrigerator if you plan to use up within a few days as soup or as an ingredient in sauces and stews; otherwise, freeze in convenient small freezer containers for easy thawing. Makes about 3½ quarts.

Chicken Stock

I've used chicken here, but this recipe is equally successful with turkey, goose, or duck, whose stock will not be clear, but may be used in gravies or cream soups.

SIMMERING TIME: 10 MINUTES
COOKER TIME: 2 TO 3 HOURS

Giblets, neck, and wing tips of 1 chicken
Carcass of 1 roast chicken
2 quarts cold water
1 large carrot
1 outside stalk celery
Celery tops, if available
1 medium onion, unpeeled
1 sprig parsley
1 sprig fresh thyme or a pinch of dried thyme

½ bay leaf
3 peppercorns
1 teaspoon salt

Place chicken parts and carcass in 4-quart kettle with 2 quarts cold water, boil for 3 minutes, then drain and discard water. Refill with 2 more quarts cold water, return to boiling, and add remaining ingredients. Cover, reduce heat, simmer for 10 minutes, and place in cooker for 2 to 3 hours. Skim fat off surface and discard or save for cooking. Strain stock from solids through sieve and correct stock's seasoning. Cut usable pieces of meat and vegetables into bite-size pieces, discarding the rest, and add to stock before serving as soup. If stock is to be used in cooking, save only liquid, and refrigerate or freeze at once in 1- to 2-cup containers. Serves 6.

New House Soup

So-called because we bring this soup as a neighborly gift to newlyweds or people moving into a new home, where cooking a meal can be difficult until things have settled down in the kitchen.

SIMMERING TIME: 20 MINUTES
COOKER TIME: 2 HOURS (DO NOT EXTEND THE COOKER TIME)

1 chicken, cut into serving pieces (for an old tough hen, increase simmering time to 30 minutes)
½ cup thin noodles
½ cup rice
1 cup carrots, halved lengthwise, then cut into 2-inch
pieces
1 large onion, sliced
2 cloves garlic, peeled and halved
1 small cauliflower, cut into flowerets
3 large leaves Savoy cabbage (in season), coarsely chopped
1 green pepper, cut into 2-inch chunks
3 quarts water or chicken broth
3 teaspoons salt
1 teaspoon caraway seeds
Pepper to taste
1 cup fresh peas, shelled
Chopped parsley for garnish

In 6-quart pot bring water to boil. Add chicken pieces (including neck and gizzard), bring again to boil, and cover. Reduce heat and simmer for 15 minutes. Add all other ingredients except peas and parsley, and bring again to boil. Cover, reduce heat, and simmer for 5 minutes more. Place in fireless cooker for 2 hours. At serving time, bring to boil, add peas, simmer long enough to cook peas, correct seasoning, and garnish with chopped parsley. Serves 6.

Note: This meal is very good when first cooked, but does not lend itself to warming over or freezing because the rice and noodles get mushy. Plan so most of it will be eaten, or leave the rice out, or separate the rice from the rest of the meal before refrigerating.

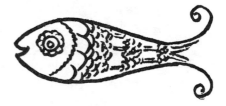

Bouillabaisse

If you follow this recipe up until the time you add the fish and shellfish, you will have a delicious fish stock. Add fish or shellfish 10 to 15 minutes before serving, cook only until tender, and you'll have a good Bouillabaisse.

SIMMERING TIME: 10 MINUTES
COOKER TIME: 2 HOURS

> 4 pounds fish and shellfish (use 2 or 3 different types of whole fish, plus crab, clams, mussels, or whatever, in the shell)
> 2 tablespoons cooking fat
> 4 cloves garlic, peeled and halved
> 1 large onion, chopped

1 large carrot, chopped
1 stalk celery, chopped
4 leeks, sliced
4 tomatoes or canned equivalent, quartered
2 tablespoons fresh rosemary (2 teaspoons dried)
2 tablespoons fresh oregano (2 teaspoons dried)
2 tablespoons fresh fennel (2 teaspoons dried)
1 teaspoon saffron
Salt and pepper to taste
6 cups water or broth
½ cup dry white wine
1 to 2 tablespoons white vinegar (optional)
Parsley, chopped, for garnish
Chives, chopped, for garnish

Clean and cut fish and shellfish into serving-size pieces; do not discard heads, tails, fins, or trimmings. Refrigerate cleaned pieces. In 4½-quart pot, melt cooking fat and sauté garlic, vegetables, herbs, and saffron over medium heat, stirring gently for 2 to 3 minutes. Add fish heads and other trimmings, plus salt and pepper. Add water, wine, and vinegar, and bring to boil. Cover, reduce heat, and simmer for 10 minutes. Place in fireless cooker for 2 hours. Twenty minutes before serving, strain stock, and add fish and crab pieces. Simmer 10 minutes more, add remaining shellfish, and simmer only 5 minutes more. Fish should be done but not overdone, and shellfish should be opened. Garnish with parsley and chives, and serve with garlic bread. Serves 6 to 8 for dinner.

Cream of Vegetable Soup

SIMMERING TIME: 2 MINUTES
COOKER TIME: 1 HOUR

> 5 tablespoons flour
> 5 tablespoons butter or cooking fat
> 1 cup fresh vegetables, cut into bite-size pieces
> 1 quart cold water, chicken broth, skim milk, or water
>   saved from cooking vegetables, or any combination
>   of these
> Salt and pepper to taste

In 2-quart pot, brown flour in butter over medium heat, and add fresh vegetables. Sauté about 2 minutes and remove from heat. Add liquid gradually, return to heat, and stir rapidly until smooth. Season to taste with salt and pepper and bring to boil. Cover, reduce heat, and simmer for 2 minutes. Place in fireless cooker for 1 hour. Serves 4 to 6.

Cream of Cauliflower Soup

Follow Cream of Vegetable Soup recipe, using half a medium-size cauliflower, broken or cut into bite-size flowerets, for fresh vegetable. Serves 4 to 6.

Variation: Cook cauliflower in advance, using liquid in which it was cooked as part of liquid for cream-soup base, then add cooked flowerets to be heated in soup at serving time.

Brown Onion Soup

Follow Cream of Vegetable Soup recipe, using half a large onion, sliced, as the only vegetable. Brown mixture until flour is very brown, and onion is brown but not burned. Serves 4 to 6.

Savoy Cabbage Soup

Follow Cream of Vegetable Soup recipe, adding at browning stage 1 cup Savoy cabbage, cut into ½-inch-by-2-inch strips, or coarsely chopped. Add 1 teaspoon caraway seeds. Serves 4 to 6.

Variation #1: Add 1 medium diced, raw potato after liquid has been added.

Variation #2: Add cooked rice to be heated in soup at serving time.

Variation #3: To variations 1 or 2, add bite-size slices of fully cooked sausage at serving time for a one-dish meal. Serve with croutons.

Potato Soup

SIMMERING TIME: 5 MINUTES
COOKER TIME: 1 TO 2 HOURS

        1 quart water or broth
        2 large potatoes, diced
        4 slices bacon or salt port, diced (for vegetarian soup,
            substitute 2 tablespoons any cooking fat)
        1 medium onion, chopped
        1 medium carrot, sliced
        1 stalk celery, sliced
        1 small green pepper, in 1-inch chunks
        2 cloves garlic, peeled and minced
        1 teaspoon caraway seeds
        1 to 2 tablespoons fresh or 1 teaspoon dried rosemary,
            savory, or thyme (optional)
        2 tablespoons flour
        1 tablespoon paprika
        Salt and pepper to taste

In 3-quart pot, bring water to boil. Add potatoes, reduce heat, and simmer for 5 minutes. In the meantime, in a frying pan, fry bacon and add vegetables, garlic, and caraway seeds. Sauté over medium heat until onions are transparent; add herbs if desired. Add flour, stir and brown a little, and remove pot from heat. Add potatoes with water in which they were boiled, and stir

rapidly to avoid lumps. Return soup to heating unit. Add paprika, adjust seasonings, and bring again to boiling point. Cover, reduce heat, and simmer for 5 minutes. Place in fireless cooker for 1 to 2 hours. Serves 4 to 6.

Note: Other vegetables may be added as the seasons change. I particularly like to add Savoy cabbage when it is available.

Variation: To make vichyssoise, follow this recipe, omitting onion, carrot, celery, and green pepper. Halve 3 leeks lengthwise, clean thoroughly in large bowl of water, then cut into 1-inch pieces. Complete as in Potato Soup, and serve hot or chilled.

Minestrone

SIMMERING TIME: 10 TO 20 MINUTES
COOKER TIME: 4 TO 5 HOURS

½ cup small dry white beans
4 cups boiling water

2 cups broth
½ cup carrots
½ cup celery
½ cup zucchini
½ cup peas
½ cup sliced onion
4 large tomatoes, quartered
¼ teaspoon pepper
½ bay leaf
⅔ cup noodles or other pasta, broken into bite-size pieces

Bring beans to boil in water and soak for 2 hours, or soak in cold water overnight. In the morning, bring beans and water to boil in 3-quart pot, cover, reduce heat, and simmer for 10 minutes (or 20 minutes if beans are long-cooking variety). Place in fireless cooker for 4 to 5 hours. About 15 minutes before serving time, remove bay leaf, and, if you wish, put bean-and-water mixture into blender and whirl at medium speed until smooth, or pass through sieve. Add all other ingredients and boil gently until vegetables are done, about 10 minutes. Serves 6.

Variation: Delete noodles and substitute ¾ cup cooked rice; add only a few minutes before serving time to prevent from getting mushy.

BORSCHT—A SOUP OR A DINNER

There are as many different kinds of borscht as there are nationalities and ethnic groups in the upper right corner of the map of Central Europe. To some, borscht is a beet-red soup served cold with sour cream and cold diced potatoes. In the U.S., if it's on the menu at all, it is likely to come from a jar, taste watery, and contain a few pale strips of floating beets that have been cooked to death.

If you go to a Russian or Polish or Jewish restaurant, things will be very different. There'll be many variations (made with duck, ham and other meats) but still the cook will insist he is making genuine borscht. It is usually served hot, with sour cream and cold diced potatoes, as a rich, gloriously red soup with meat and all kinds of vegetables in it. You can surely call this dinner at its very best.

The following adaptation of what a Czech cook made for my Polish father is easy, is delicious hot or cold, and is a complete dinner.

51

Borscht

SIMMERING TIME: 20 MINUTES
COOKER TIME: 3 TO 4 HOURS

2- to 3-pound pot roast, boned (save bones for broth)
2 quarts water
1 celeriac (celery root), if available
1 large onion, quartered
4 large beets or equivalent amount of small beets
4 large carrots
Young and tender beet greens, or 4 Savoy cabbage
    leaves, in 2-inch sections
4 medium-size potatoes, cooked, peeled and diced
2 cups sour cream
1½ teaspoons salt
1 teaspoon caraway seed
¼ teaspoon pepper

In 6-quart pot, bring cold water to boil together with bones. Add beef, return to boil, cover, reduce heat, and simmer for 15 minutes. Add vegetables and seasonings, bring again to boil; cover and reduce heat to simmer for 5 minutes. Place in fireless cooker for 3 hours. At serving time, remove beets, add beet greens, and boil for 5 minutes. Peel and cut beets into quarters or wedges, depending on size, cut meat into chunks or slices, and return beets and meat to broth. Top off each bowl of borscht with cooled, diced potatoes and sour cream. Serves 6.

Lentil Soup

SIMMERING TIME: 10 MINUTES
COOKER TIME: 3 TO 4 HOURS

1 cup lentils
5 cups cold water
¼ pound salt pork, diced
1 large onion, chopped
1 clove garlic, minced
1 small green pepper, cut into 1-inch pieces
2 tomatoes, quartered, or canned equivalent
½ teaspoon salt
¼ teaspoon pepper
1 tablespoon paprika
1 tablespoon butter or cooking fat
1 tablespoon flour for thickening
½ cup cold water or broth
2 to 3 teaspoons lemon juice or to taste
Croutons

Soak lentils in cold water in 3-quart pot. (Some lentils don't require soaking; check package's instructions). Fry salt pork until golden brown, lift cracklings out of fat, and set aside. Sauté vegetables in remaining fat over medium heat for about 2 or 3 minutes, or until onions are transparent. Add water that lentils were soaked in, lentils, and seasonings, and bring to boil in 3-

quart pot, reduce heat, cover, and simmer for 10 minutes. Place in cooker for 3 to 4 hours. At serving time melt butter in small frying pan, add flour, and stir until lightly browned. Remove from heat, stir in a little cold water, return to heat, and gradually add rest of water. Bring lentil soup to boil, slowly stir in thickening mixture, and simmer for 5 to 7 minutes. Add lemon juice and reserved salt pork cracklings and serve soup with croutons. Serves 4 to 6.

Note: To make a thicker soup, increase the flour and butter for the thickening or add a large peeled and grated potato to the mixture at the start of the simmering time, before you place it in the cooker.

Split Pea Soup

SIMMERING TIME: 10 MINUTES
COOKER TIME: 3 TO 4 HOURS

> 1 cup split peas
> 5 cups cold water
> 3 medium carrots, cut into 1-inch pieces
> 1 medium onion, sliced
> 1 stalk celery, cut into 1-inch slices
> 1 outside cabbage leaf, if available, chopped
> 2 tablespoons any cooking fat

1 tablespoon fresh or 1 teaspoon dried rosemary, sage,
   or oregano
1 pound ham shank, or ½ cup coarsely chopped ham,
   or ½ cup fried bacon ends (optional)
¼ teaspoon pepper
1 tablespoon paprika
1 tablespoon butter
1 tablespoon flour
1 cup milk
Salt to taste
Chopped chives or parsley, for garnish

Soak peas in cold water for 2 hours in 3-quart pot. Sauté vegetables in fat over medium heat for 3 or 4 minutes or until onion is transparent; add herbs and sauté 1 more minute. Add water that peas were soaked in, or substitute broth for some of it if no meat will be used. Stir and add peas, meat, pepper, and paprika. Bring to boil, cover, reduce heat, simmer for 10 minutes, and place in cooker for 3 to 4 hours. At serving time melt butter in small frying pan, add flour, and stir 2 to 3 minutes. Remove from heat, and stir in small amount of milk, return to medium heat, and gradually stir in rest of milk. Bring soup to boil and add thickening mixture gradually. Add salt to taste, cover, and simmer soup for 5 to 7 minutes. Garnish with chopped chives or parsley and serve with croutons. Serves 4 to 6.

Note: If a thicker soup is desired, increase the amount of butter and flour for thickening. If you prefer your pea soup puréed, lift the meat out of the soup with a slotted spoon before puréeing soup in blender or passing it through a sieve. Split peas can also be served as a vegetable. They are very good in winter or whenever there are no fresh vegetables available, served with ham, pork, or sausage cooked with the peas or heated in the pea mixture at serving time. Use the above recipe, but reduce the amount of liquid used by 1 or 2 cups, depending on the consistency you like. A large peeled and grated potato can be added before simmering, as thickening, to substitute for the flour and butter.

Grains and Cereals

All grains lend themselves to cooking in the fireless cooker: the slow cooking method improves texture and flavor, and simmering time on the stove is short, avoiding burning and the need for a double boiler.

Most grains can be prepared in the accustomed way with one exception: grains cooked in the fireless cooker will require somewhat less water than would be needed for stove-top cooking, because once the cereal is in the cooker, no water loss occurs as it does on the stove, when steam escapes along the crack of the lid. For instance, the standard method for cooking oatmeal would be to allow 2 cups of water for 1 cup of oatmeal. In the fireless cooker, you need only 1¾ cups water for each cup of oatmeal.

Grains and legumes, a particularly good addition to vegetarian diets because of their nutritional value, can be successfully cooked together in the fireless cooker. After soaking a legume (see next chapter) I cook it with the grain and use the simmering time suggested for the legume—15 minutes for beans that require medium-long cooking periods. (Soy beans and some other legumes with particularly long cooking requirements do better if they go through the simmering and cooker processes twice.) A particularly good combination is white beans and barley. Other vegetables can be added for the last 5 minutes of the simmering time, then placed in the cooker for several hours.

Cereal for breakfast can be cooked overnight in the fireless cooker if the quantity needed is at least 1½ to 2 quarts. Smaller amounts will get done just as well but may cool off after that many hours and would have to be rewarmed.

Some cereals have short cooker periods—Cornmeal Mush, for example. If one member of the family gets up earlier than the others and simmers the cereal for 2 minutes and puts it in the cooker, it will be ready for the rest of the family in an hour.

Rice

Most of the time, I use standard long-grain white rice or brown rice, in the usual proportions of 1 cup of rice to 2 cups of water or broth. Prepackaged rice is clean and free of foreign matter, and I am not in the habit of washing it. There are many different types of rice on the market, some of which require washing or different proportions of rice and water. I have no experience with these and suggest you experiment if the standard method does not work. Rice is a particularly suitable food for preparing in the fireless cooker and I would hate to think of anyone giving it up just because one type of rice requires somewhat different handling.

1½ cups long-grain white or standard brown rice
2 tablespoons cooking fat
3 cups water or broth
1 small onion, peeled
1 teaspoon salt

In 2-quart pot, fry rice briefly in fat or until a few grains turn white or translucent. Add water and onion, and bring to boil; cover, reduce heat, and simmer for 5 minutes. Place in fireless cooker for 1 to 2 hours. Serves 4 to 6.

Note: If you want to use the rice as a cereal with milk or to make a rice pudding, omit the onion and use water. For any dish, I prefer to use the brief frying method because it prevents the rice from turning mushy. But other methods work too.

Tarhonya (Mock Barley)

Tarhonya is a noodle-type product available in stores featuring Italian specialties. There it is known as *grandini* or mock barley. It can also be made at home, but I prefer to buy it ready-made and save the labor.

SIMMERING TIME: 5 MINUTES
COOKER TIME: 1 TO 2 HOURS

3 slices bacon, diced
1 small onion, chopped
1 clove garlic, minced
1½ cup tarhonya (mock barley)
2 tablespoons paprika
3 cups water or broth
Parsley, chopped, for garnish

In 2-quart pot, fry bacon until crisp; add chopped onion and garlic, and fry gently until transparent. Add tarhonya and fry 1 minute, stirring constantly.

Remove from heat while stirring in paprika (this precaution is important because paprika will turn bitter if temperature is too high). Add water, stir, and return to heating unit. Bring to boil, cover, reduce heat, and simmer for 5 minutes. Place in fireless cooker for 1 to 2 hours. At serving time stir and sprinkle with chopped parsley. Serve tarhonya with goulash or any other stew or gravy. Serves 6.

Note: If you prefer noodle-type products soft rather than *al dente,* add an extra ¼ cup of water. This will make the tarhonya texture softer and fluffier.

Oatmeal

SIMMERING TIME: 5 MINUTES
COOKER TIME: 1 TO 2 HOURS

   2 cups long-cooking oatmeal
   3 tablespoons butter or margarine
   3 cups water
   1 teaspoon salt

In 2-quart pot, fry oatmeal briefly in butter, add water and salt, and bring to boil. Cover, reduce heat, simmer for 5 minutes, and place in fireless cooker for 1 to 2 hours. I fry oatmeal before boiling because we like it somewhat grainy. If you prefer smooth oatmeal, omit frying. Serves 6.

Cornmeal Mush

SIMMERING TIME: 1 MINUTE
COOKER TIME: 1 HOUR

   3 cups cold water
   1 cup cornmeal
   1 teaspoon salt

Stir 1 cup water into cornmeal. Add salt to rest of water and bring to boil. Gradually add cornmeal and cold-water mixture to boiling water so that water continues to boil as you stir it in. Cover, reduce heat to simmer for 1 minute, and place in fireless cooker for 1 hour. Serves 6.

Polenta

SIMMERING TIME: 1 MINUTE
COOKER TIME: 1 HOUR

1 cup cornmeal
3 cups cold water
1 teaspoon salt
½ cup grated Parmesan cheese
2 tablespoons butter

Prepare Cornmeal Mush (preceding). Add cheese, stir well, cool 1 hour in refrigerator, slice, and fry in butter. Serves 6.

Variation #1: Set Cornmeal Mush aside to cool without adding Parmesan cheese, then fry it, sliced, in butter, and sprinkle Parmesan cheese over each helping.

Variation #2: Cool and slice Cornmeal Mush, then roll in beaten egg and bread crumbs. Fry in butter on both sides until golden.

Polenta and Carrots

SIMMERING TIME: 1 MINUTE
COOKER TIME: 1 HOUR

1 cup cornmeal
3 cups cold water
1 teaspoon salt
12 small young carrots, left whole, or 6 medium carrots,
   cut into 2-inch strips
2 tablespoons butter or other cooking fat

Prepare Cornmeal Mush, cool and cut into strips about 1 by 2 inches. Sauté in butter with carrots until carrots are tender and polenta strips are crisp and golden brown. Serves 6.

Variation #1: Other vegetables can be added to carrots or substituted for them. Green pepper chunks, coarsely chopped outer leaves of cabbage, and small onions are particularly good and add to color appeal of this good fast lunch or vegetarian dinner dish.

Legumes (Dried Beans, Lentils, and Peas)

There are many varieties of legumes on the market, some of them already cooked or otherwise processed. Therefore, it is important to look carefully at the package information before buying. I prefer to buy unprocessed foods (legumes or anything else), because they are usually less expensive and go farther.

I always soak legumes before cooking. If I don't have much time, I soak them 1 hour in hot water, but I prefer to soak them in cold water 4 to 5 hours or overnight. I always soak them in the amount of water given in the recipe and then use this water in cooking, in order to avoid the loss of nutritionally important trace substances that leach into the water during the soaking period. (After soaking soy beans, however, discard the water, which will have a bitter taste, and replace it with fresh water.) I add salt to legumes just before serving because this is supposed to soften them. Since I taste all food at serving time to make sure it's done, to see that I haven't forgotten anything, and to correct the seasoning, this method works well for me.

If legumes are used either as part of a vegetarian one-dish meal or with meat, it is important to look up the simmering times of the other ingredients and act accordingly. For instance, beans require a longer simmering time (10 minutes or more) than carrots (5 minutes). Give the beans a good head start, especially if you are using long-cooking beans, and then add the other ingredients for the last 5 minutes or so. Barley and other grains combine well with legumes because of complementary nutrients and flavors.

Navy Beans

SIMMERING TIME #1: 15 MINUTES
COOKER TIME #1: 3 TO 8 HOURS
SIMMERING TIME #2: 15 MINUTES
COOKER TIME #2: 3 TO 8 HOURS

2 cups navy beans or other long-cooking beans
6 cups cold water
Salt and pepper to taste
Fried onion rings or fried bacon bits, for garnish
Parsley, chopped, for garnish
1 tablespoon paprika, for garnish (optional)

In the morning of the day *before* you plan to eat the beans, soak them in cold water in 4-quart pot. (Check package's instructions regarding cooking and soaking.) That evening, bring beans and water in which they were soaked to boil. Cover, reduce heat, and simmer for 15 minutes. Place in fireless cooker for 3 to 8 hours, then bring to boil again for 15 minutes and return pot to cooker

3 to 8 hours (all day or until serving time). At serving time, boil once again, season, and garnish. Paprika adds color and flavor.

If time is short, you can get by with a brief boil, a 1-hour soak time, and a single cooker time. But in that case, double simmering time to 20 to 30 minutes and allow 4 to 8 hours' cooker time. Plan to take them out of cooker 30 minutes before serving so you can cook them a bit longer if necessary. Serves 6.

Variation #1: Beans are also good when passed through a sieve or blended. One such old-fashioned dish is called Bean Porridge. This variation will also rescue the cook's honor if the beans turn out to be a little underdone at serving time.

Variation #2: Sausages or 1 to 2 pounds of ham hocks can be added during second simmering time.

Beans and Barley

SIMMERING TIME: 10 MINUTES
COOKER TIME: 4 TO 5 HOURS

> 1½ cups large white beans (these require less cooking
>   than other varieties, so check package instructions)
> 6 cups hot water
> ½ cup barley

Salt and pepper to taste
Bacon bits, for garnish
Parsley, chopped, for garnish

In 3-quart pot, soak white beans for an hour or more in hot water. Add barley and bring to boil. Cover and reduce heat to simmer for 10 minutes. Place in fireless cooker for 4 to 5 hours. At serving time, season and garnish. Serves 6.

Note: Carrots, green pepper, or any other vegetable may be added for color and taste (or because they need using up); leftover ham or sausage can be added for variety.

Variation: To make this dish into a soup, use 2 quarts water or broth and before serving, thicken with 2 tablespoons flour. Serve with rye bread.

Lentils

SIMMERING TIME: 10 MINUTES
COOKER TIME: 3 TO 4 HOURS

1 cup lentils
3 cups cold water
1 teaspoon salt
¼ teaspoon pepper
1 tablespoon paprika

1 tablespoon flour
3 tablespoons cold water
Chopped parsley, for garnish

Soak lentils in water for 2 hours, unless otherwise instructed on package. Add salt, pepper, and paprika, bring to boil in soaking water, and cover. Reduce heat, simmer for 10 minutes, then place in cooker for 3 to 4 hours. Gradually bring again to boil, add flour dissolved in cold water, and simmer for 5 minutes. Correct seasonings and serve garnished with parsley. Serves 6.

Note: Before the thickening is added, some of the lentils can be set aside for a salad. Lentil salad is best if served with Vinaigrette Dressing made with lemon rather than vinegar and garnished with chopped onion, parsley, and bacon bits.

Meats and One-Dish Meals

A juicy, tender cut of meat will always have a better chance of producing a superior meal, particularly if it is beef. But a less prestigious cut of meat, if prepared appropriately in the fireless cooker, will produce wonderful food, too. The very toughest meats, such as beef heart and tongue, require two simmerings and two sessions in the cooker to become tender, but they can be prepared with much less work and much less fuel than traditional methods demand.

Plain Boiled Beef

SIMMERING TIME: 20 TO 30 MINUTES

COOKER TIME: 3 TO 5 HOURS

1 to 2 pounds marrow bone
2 quarts cold water, broth, or vegetable water
2 to 3 pounds chuck roast or other beef, no more than
   3 inches thick
2 cloves garlic, crushed
1 teaspoon caraway seeds
1 large onion, with some of the dry outer leaves left on
1 celeriac (celery root), about 1 to 1½ pounds, well
   scrubbed and cut in half

2 teaspoons salt
1 parsley root, if available
6 large carrots
½ Savoy cabbage, about 1 pound, cut in wedges
Salt and pepper to taste
Chopped parsley for garnish

In 6-quart pot bring marrow bones and water to boil. Add meat, garlic, caraway seeds, onion, celeriac, and salt. Bring again to boil, cover, reduce heat, and simmer for 15 minutes. Add remaining vegetables and seasonings. Cover, return to boil, reduce heat to simmer for 5 more minutes, and place pot in fireless cooker for 3 to 5 hours, depending on quality of meat. If you are not sure of quality of meat, be sure to allow plenty of cooker time. Test meat with fork for tenderness about 1 hour before serving. If done, bring again to boil and replace in cooker; if less than tender, give second simmering time of 5 to 10 minutes and replace in cooker. At serving time slice across grain of meat and arrange on platter. Pour small amount of seasoned broth over slices. Serve broth with meat course, in cups garnished with chopped parsley. Arrange vegetables attractively on platter around meat. Serves 6 generously.

Note: Some people add peeled potatoes to make a one-dish meal. I prefer to prepare the potatoes in another cooker and serve them separately. Prepared horseradish, good mustard, and dill pickles are traditionally served with this meal. Or prepare a sauce made of 1 cup applesauce mixed with 2 teaspoons prepared horseradish. The freshly cooked bone marrow, when spread on rye bread and salted, is a great delicacy.

Variation: This becomes Fancy Boiled Beef if a better cut of beef is used and chicken wings, backs, and gizzards are added. Discard chicken parts and vegetables before serving broth.

Corned Beef

SIMMERING TIME # 1: 20 MINUTES
COOKER TIME # 1: 4 HOURS OR OVERNIGHT
SIMMERING TIME # 2: 10 MINUTES
COOKER TIME # 2: 4 HOURS OR ALL DAY

2 to 3 pounds corned beef, rinsed in cold water or briefly parboiled
2 quarts cold water, or enough to fill pot two-thirds full
1 bay leaf

Wipe corned beef dry and place in 4-quart pot. Add water and bay leaf, and bring to boil. Cover, reduce heat, simmer for 20 minutes, and place in fireless cooker for 4 hours or overnight. Return pot to stove to boil again, and simmer for 10 minutes. Return to fireless cooker for 4 hours or all day. Before serving, bring again to boil, then simmer for several minutes.

Slice and serve with mashed potatoes or dried beans cooked separately. Serves 6 generously.

Variation: Cook corned beef together with beans, but omit salt.

Boiled Corned Beef and Cabbage

SIMMERING TIME # 1: 30 MINUTES
COOKER TIME # 1: 3 TO 4 HOURS
SIMMERING TIME # 2: 5 TO 10 MINUTES
COOKER TIME # 2: 3 TO 4 HOURS

Either cooker time can be all day or all night. In such a case, immediately before serving, bring food to boil and simmer 5 minutes.

2 to 3 pounds corned beef brisket or similar cut
Cold water, for washing
2 quarts cold water, for cooking
1 teaspoon peppercorns
1 teaspoon caraway seeds
½ head Savoy cabbage or white cabbage, about 1 pound, cut in wedges or coarsely chopped
6 medium carrots
1 medium onion, peeled (save some of the dry, brown skin to add to broth)

Wash corned beef in cold water and wipe. If you want to remove more salt, cover corned beef with cold water and bring to boil; discard water. In 6-quart pot, combine corned beef with enough cold water to fill pot two-thirds full, and bring to boil. Add peppercorns and caraway seeds, cover, reduce heat, and simmer for 30 minutes; place in fireless cooker for 3 to 4 hours. Return pot to stove and test meat for doneness with large fork. Normally, it will be slightly underdone at this stage, giving some resistance as fork is inserted and removed. Bring meat and broth back to boil, add cabbage, carrots, onion, and onion skin, and return broth to boiling. Cover, reduce heat, and simmer for 5 to 10 minutes, depending on how well done meat was when tested, and return to fireless cooker for 3 to 4 hours more.

At serving time, drain meat and vegetables, reserving broth for use at this meal or at some later time. (The broth is mild, not too salty, and has a delicious flavor that older people remember nostalgically from turn-of-the-century-style cooking.) Slice corned beef, arrange attractively on platter, and surround with vegetables. Serve with mustard or horseradish, or with Viennese-style sauce made from mixing 1 cup applesauce with 2 teaspoons prepared horseradish. Dumplings or potatoes make a good side dish. One advantage of this dish is that it's very good when reheated. Serves 8 generously.

Variation: Six to 8 medium potatoes, peeled and quartered lengthwise, may be added for last 2 to 3 minutes of *second* simmering time. Make sure broth returns to boiling, then cover and place in cooker for 3 to 4 hours, as above. Potatoes will be quite tender and will have a slight thickening effect on broth. Serve as above; garnishing potatoes with chopped parsley will add an elegant touch.

Sauerbraten

My older daughter, Ronnie, has adapted this old favorite for the fireless cooker.

SIMMERING TIME: 20 TO 30 MINUTES
COOKER TIME: 4 TO 5 HOURS

3 to 4 pounds beef (bottom round, chuck, or brisket)
½ cup vinegar or red wine
Water, to fill pot two-thirds full
1 large onion, sliced
2 large carrots, sliced
½ cup parsley, chopped
2 cloves garlic
1 bay leaf
10 peppercorns
1 teaspoon salt
2 tablespoons cooking fat, for browning meat
2 tablespoons flour
2 tablespoons cooking fat, for browning flour

Salt and pepper to taste
Parsley sprigs for garnish

Soak beef overnight in vinegar and water, along with onion, carrots, parsley, spices, and seasonings; store in refrigerator. Next day drain, reserving marinade for use in gravy. Brown meat in fat in 4-quart pot. In the meantime, in a different pan, brown flour in fat until quite dark brown. Remove from heat and gradually stir in some of reserved marinade. Combine all ingredients in pot and stir in rest of reserved marinade. Pot should be two-thirds full; add or remove liquid if necessary. Bring to boil, cover, reduce heat, and simmer for 20 to 30 minutes. Place in fireless cooker for 4 to 5 hours. At serving time, bring again to boil, simmer for 5 minutes; correct seasoning, slice meat, pass gravy through strainer, and serve with meat. Some people would discard carrots and onion along with bay leaf and other spices in marinade; I like to decorate the platter of meat with carrots, onion, and sprigs of parsley. Serves 8 generously.

Note: Sauerbraten goes well with Dumpling in a Napkin, Tarhonya, or Little Steamed Dumplings. If time is short, plain rice or noodles will do.

Pot Roast

SIMMERING TIME: 20 TO 30 MINUTES
COOKER TIME: 3 TO 5 HOURS

2 tablespoons flour
1 teaspoon salt
¼ teaspoon pepper
2 to 3 pounds pot roast (chuck or rump)
2 tablespoons butter or shortening

½ teaspoon sugar
1 onion, sliced
2 cups broth or water
2 carrots, cut into 2-inch pieces
1 stalk celery, cut into 2-inch pieces
2 tablespoons flour or 2 teaspoons cornstarch
2 tablespoons cold water

Mix flour and seasonings and roll meat in this mixture. Melt butter in 3-quart pot, add sugar, and brown meat slowly but thoroughly on all sides. Add onion and liquid and bring to boil. Cover, reduce heat, and simmer for 15 minutes. Add carrots and celery and bring again to boil. Cover, reduce heat to simmer 5 minutes more, and place in fireless cooker for 3 to 5 hours. At serving time, bring to boil, simmer for 5 minutes; correct seasoning. To thicken gravy, rapidly beat cold water into flour with fork; add this mixture to liquid while stirring, and bring to boil briefly. Slice meat and serve with gravy, plus rice, potatoes, or dumplings. Serves 6.

Note: Potatoes cut into 1½-inch cubes can be added about 7 to 10 minutes before serving and simmered; if added at simmering time, they easily get overdone.

Meatballs and Gravy

SIMMERING TIME: 10 MINUTES
COOKER TIME: 2 HOURS

1 cup bread crumbs
¼ cup milk or water
1 small onion, chopped
1 clove garlic, minced
1 tablespoon fresh or 1 teaspoon dried rosemary,
    thyme, or other herb
1 teaspoon salt
¼ teaspoon pepper
1 tablespoon paprika
1½ pounds lean ground beef
2 tablespoons cooking fat
5 tablespoons flour mixed with cold water
2 large tomatoes, cut into wedges
3 cups broth or water

Soak bread crumbs in milk, then add onion, garlic, herbs, seasonings, and ground beef; mix well. Shape mixture into meatballs about 1 or 2 inches in diameter. Brown meatballs on all
sides in fat. Mix flour with cold water and stir with fork until
smooth. Combine with broth and tomatoes in 3-quart pot and
bring to boil. Add meatballs, and return to boil. Cover, reduce

heat, simmer for 10 minutes, and place in cooker for 2 hours. At serving time, bring to boil and simmer 5 minutes; if necessary, correct thickness of gravy. Serves 6.

Pork Patties in Tomato Sauce

SIMMERING TIME: 10 MINUTES
COOKER TIME: 2 HOURS

1 cup bread crumbs
¼ cup milk
1 teaspoon dried herbs
1 teaspoon salt
¼ teaspoon pepper
1 hot chile pepper, ground (optional)
1½ pounds ground pork
2 cups broth
1 6-ounce can tomato sauce
2 tablespoons flour

Soak bread crumbs in milk, add herbs, seasonings, chile pepper, and pork; mix well. Shape into 1- to 2-inch patties or into 2-by-½-inch oblong "little pigs." Brown on all sides in skillet, removing fat as it accumulates. In the meantime, bring broth and tomato sauce to boil in 2-quart pot. Add pork patties, return to boil, and cover. Reduce heat, simmer for 10 minutes, and place in fireless cooker for 2 hours. At serving time, bring to boil and simmer for 5 minutes; correct seasoning and thicken with flour (flour may also be added just before simmering time). Serves 6.

SAUERKRAUT: IT NEEDN'T BE OVERWHELMING

Sauerkraut or any other salty food can be made less salty by simply washing it in cold water; for many people's taste, this is enough. There are, however, ways to make it even milder. First washing, then soaking sauerkraut in cold water is one. Draining the juice (to be reserved for later use), then pouring boiling water over the sauerkraut is another, made even more effective by letting the kraut stand in the hot water. Some people parboil sauerkraut for 5 to 10 minutes, then drain it, but by that time too much of the flavor and food value has been leached out. With any of these methods, additional mildness can be achieved with long, slow cooking, as in the fireless cooker.

Other foods that improve with desalination are corned beef, pickled tongue, and smoked pork ribs. But desalination never removes all the salt, so a person on a low-salt diet should avoid salt-cured foods altogether, and young children should be given small helpings and more fluids than usual. I suggest omitting salt in all recipes containing sauerkraut and using only other seasonings.

Pork and Sauerkraut

SIMMERING TIME: 20 MINUTES
COOKER TIME: 3 TO 4 HOURS

1½ pounds pork shoulder, trimmed and cut into 1-inch cubes
1 onion, chopped or sliced
1 quart sauerkraut, fresh or canned
2 to 2½ cups liquid (half sauerkraut juice and half water)
Pepper or cayenne to taste
2 tablespoons paprika
1 apple, grated (optional)
1 medium potato, grated
1 green pepper, cut into 2-inch pieces
3 tablespoons sour cream, for garnish

In 3-quart pot, gently render pork fat trimmed from shoulder, add onion and meat, and sauté briefly over medium heat. In the meantime, drain and desalinate sauerkraut (see page 00), reserving about 1¼ cups of liquid (less if you want a mild flavor). Add sauerkraut and liquid to meat and onion, add seasonings, and bring to boil. Cover, reduce heat, and simmer for 20 minutes, adding apple, potato, and green pepper for last 5 minutes of simmering. Place in fireless cooker for 3 to 4 hours. Garnish with sour cream and serve with boiled potatoes or dumplings. Serves 6.

Cabbage Rolls

SIMMERING TIME: 10 MINUTES
COOKER TIME: 2 TO 3 HOURS

8 large outside leaves Savoy cabbage or other cabbage
2 quarts water, for boiling cabbage leaves
¾ pound ground beef
¾ pound ground pork
1 large onion, chopped
1 teaspoon fresh oregano, finely minced, or equivalent
   dried
1 teaspoon fresh rosemary, finely minced, or equivalent
   dried
Salt and pepper to taste
Paprika to taste (optional)
4 large tomatoes, cut into wedges
2 cups broth or water used to cook cabbage
1 cup beer

Remove tough stems from cabbage leaves and boil leaves in water until soft and pliable, about 7 minutes. In the meantime, fry meat in skillet, removing excess fat. Add onion, herbs, and seasonings, and gently cook until onion is transparent. Divide mixture into 8 parts, spoon onto each cabbage leaf, and form 8 oblong 1-inch rolls, turning in ends and securing them with toothpicks. Bring tomatoes, broth, and beer to boil in 3-quart pot. Add cabbage rolls, cover, and simmer for 10 minutes. Place in fireless cooker for 2 to 3 hours. At serving time, bring to boil and simmer 5 minutes; correct seasoning. Serves 6.

Variation: Substitute 1 quart of sauerkraut for broth and beer.

Serendipity Chili

My older son, Chris, developed this version of an old favorite for the fireless cooker. Although it can be done more quickly (see Variation), the long way takes several days. Like most stews, chili gets better when it's rewarmed; in fact, the idea of this approach is to get the effect of multiple cookings.

SIMMERING TIME: 5 TO 15 MINUTES (DEPENDING ON BEANS' TENDERNESS)
COOKER TIME: 4 HOURS
May need second simmering and cooker time

> 2 cups dried pinto, kidney, or any large dark beans
> Water, for soaking and fermenting beans
> 2 tablespoons cooking fat, for sauteing vegetables
> ½ cup chopped green pepper
> 1 medium onion, chopped
> 1 clove garlic, minced
> ½ cup chopped celery, from leafy end

1 teaspoon salt
½ teaspoon freshly ground pepper
1 to 2 pounds ground beef, "chili beef," or any type of
    beef, lamb, or game, cut into 1-inch or smaller cubes
1½ teaspoons ground coffee (any grind)
½ bay leaf
2 to 6 teaspoons chili powder (depending on your taste
    and its strength)
1 teaspoon cumin
1 6-ounce can tomato paste
1 to 2 cups stewed tomatoes
Seasonings to taste

Wash and cull beans, cover with cold water, and soak overnight without lid in order to expose them to natural yeasts from the air. In the morning add water to cover, if necessary, and put lid on pot. Continue soaking until froth and odor of yeast and alcohol show that fermentation has occurred. This may take 36 to 72 hours, depending on temperature. Transfer beans to 4-quart pot, boil 5 minutes, cover, and set aside to soak in same water for 12 hours. Repeat boiling and 12-hour soaking once or twice until beans are dark brown and softened.

Melt fat, sauté vegetables briefly until onions are transparent, add meat and brown well on all sides. While meat is browning, add coffee; then add spices and tomato paste, stir, and combine with beans and soaking water. Bring to boil, cover, reduce heat, simmer for 15 minutes, and place in cooker for 4 hours. At serving time bring again to boil, correct seasoning, add garnish and, if you wish, freshly sautéed vegetables, because original vegetables have faded out of sight by now. Serves 8.

Note: Did someone wonder about the name Serendipity Chili? Well, there are two reasons for it—the coffee and the slight fermenting of the beans—both of which I discovered by accident. The first time I made chili, I was cooking for about 25 people and was starting the chili along with breakfast, so I had no time to spare. There was a cannister of coffee on the shelf above the stove where I was browning the meat. The coffee spilled into the pan, but I couldn't start over. The beans I'd put in to soak a couple of days before and forgotten about, were fermented by the time I remembered them. As it turned out, I got many compliments on that chili.

Variation: If you have only a day to make chili, just boil beans briefly in 7 cups of water, soak in same water for 1 hour, and simmer gently for about 30 minutes, also in same water. Add all other ingredients for last 15 minutes of simmering time and put into cooker for 4 to 8 hours. At serving time bring again to boil and simmer for 5 to 7 minutes. Garnish as above.

Basic Fricassee

Fricassees, which are easy and have short cooker times, would be good for learing how to use the fireless cooker.

SIMMERING TIME (STARTING AFTER ALL BASIC INGREDIENTS ARE
COMBINED): 5 MINUTES
COOKER TIME: 2 HOURS

1 tablespoon cooking oil
1 medium onion, sliced
1 clove garlic, minced
1 carrot, sliced
1 stalk celery, sliced
1½ to 2 pounds young rabbit, chicken, or veal
1 cup white wine
1 bouquet garni consisting of 1 sprig parsley, 1 sprig
   thyme, 1 sprig rosemary or other herbs, tied together
   for easy removal (or use equivalent amounts of dried
   herbs tied in small piece of cheesecloth)
Basic Fricassee Sauce (below)
Salt and pepper to taste
2 to 3 teaspoons lemon juice

Heat oil in frying pan and add onion, garlic, carrot, and celery;
sauté lightly over medium heat until onion is transparent, about
2 to 3 minutes. Lift vegetables out of pan and set aside for later
use. Lightly brown meat in oil on both sides. Add wine and bouquet garni, cover, adjust heat, and simmer for 10 minutes. In the
meantime, prepare Basic Fricassee Sauce. Add to it chicken-
wine mixture and reserved vegetables; season and stir together.
Return pot to medium heat, cover, and simmer for 5 minutes.
Place in fireless cooker for 2 hours. At serving time, bring to

boil and simmer 5 minutes. Correct seasoning, remove bouquet garni, and add lemon juice to taste. Serve with a salad and rice or noodles for an elegant meal. Serves 6.

Variation #1: Cooked meat may be substituted for the fresh meat. If I have leftover roasted chicken or lamb, I prefer to bone the meat, cut it into serving pieces about 2 inches square, and heat it to the boiling point in the wine. I omit the simmering period, which is required only for fresh meat, then combine with the sauce as above.

Variation #2: When using fresh fish, prepare fricassee sauce alone in fireless cooker as above, omitting wine. Just before serving, cut fish into 2-inch squares and simmer for 2 to 3 minutes in wine. Add fish and wine to sauce and stir.

Fricassee Sauce

   3 tablespoons butter or cooking fat
   3 tablespoons flour, or more for thicker sauce
   2 cups broth or milk
   2 egg yolks
   ¼ cup heavy cream

Melt butter in 3-quart pot, add flour, and stir. Add broth gradually, while continuing to stir over medium heat; cover, adjust heat and simmer briefly. Beat egg yolks and cream together (a wire whisk works best), then remove sauce from heat and add egg yolk–cream mixture, beating constantly until smooth, about 2 to 3 minutes.

Chicken Fricassee

*SIMMERING TIME (STARTING AFTER ALL BASIC INGREDIENTS ARE
   COMBINED): 5 MINUTES*
COOKER TIME: 2 HOURS

2 tablespoons cooking oil
1 onion, sliced
1 cup sliced mushrooms
1 clove garlic, minced or pressed
1 carrot, sliced
1 stalk celery, sliced
1 chicken, in serving-size pieces
1 cup dry white wine
1 bouquet garni (see Basic Fricassee recipe)
3 tablespoons butter or cooking fat
3 tablespoons flour, or more for thick sauce
2 cups broth, or mixture of broth and milk
2 egg yolks
¼ cup heavy cream, sour cream, or yoghurt
Salt and pepper to taste
2 to 3 teaspoons lemon juice

In a frying pan large enough to hold all chicken pieces, heat cooking oil and lightly sauté onion, mushrooms, garlic, carrot, and celery over medium heat for 2 to 3 minutes. Remove vegetables with slotted spoon and set aside for later use. Sauté chicken pieces lightly on both sides in same oil for about 2 to 3 minutes; add wine and bouquet garni, cover, reduce heat, and simmer for 10 minutes. In the meantime, prepare sauce as instructed in Basic Fricassee Sauce recipe, using butter, flour, broth, egg yolks, cream, and seasonings. In 4-quart pot, combine chicken mixture, vegetables, and sauce; bring to boil, cover, reduce heat and simmer for 5 minutes. Place in cooker for 2 hours. At serving time, remove bouquet garni, bring to boil, and simmer 5 minutes. Correct seasoning and add lemon juice to taste. Serves 6.

Variation: For Lamb Fricassee, substitute 2 pounds of lamb shoulder or neck (in 1½-inch cubes) for chicken; ¼ cup red wine for white wine; and 6-ounce can of tomato sauce for broth. Serves 6.

Basic Stew

SIMMERING TIME: 20 TO 30 MINUTES, DEPENDING ON CUT, TYPE OF
MEAT, SIZE OF PIECES, AND DESIRED DEGREE OF DONENESS
COOKER TIME: 2 TO 5 HOURS

2 tablespoons cooking fat
2 pounds pork, beef, or lamb, cut into 1½-inch cubes
2 cloves garlic, minced or pressed
2 onions, chopped
2 to 2½ cups liquid, or enough to fill pot two-thirds full
    or 2 inches from top
2 tablespoons flour, for thickening (optional)
1 to 2 cups carrots, celery, cabbage, or other vegetables,
    cut into 2-inch pieces
Salt and pepper to taste

In 3-quart pot, melt fat, and brown meat, garlic and onions over medium heat. Add liquid, bring to boil, cover, reduce heat, and simmer for 20 to 30 minutes. If using thickener, sprinkle over mixture and stir. Add vegetables. Season and bring again to boil; cover, reduce heat, and simmer for 5 minutes more. Place in fireless cooker for 2 to 5 hours. At serving time, bring to boil, and simmer 5 minutes; correct seasoning. Serves 6.

Beef Stew

SIMMERING TIME: 20 TO 30 MINUTES (DEPENDING ON CUT OF BEEF AND
   DESIRED DEGREE OF DONENESS)
COOKER TIME: 3 TO 5 HOURS

> 2 pounds stewing beef, cut into 1- or 2-inch cubes
> 2 tablespoons cooking fat
> 2 medium onions, chopped or sliced
> 4 medium carrots, cut diagonally into 2-inch pieces
> 2 large cabbage leaves, corasely chopped
> 1 stalk celery, cut into 2-inch pieces
> 2 to 3 turnips, in season, quartered or cut into 2-inch
>   cubes if large
> 2 to 2½ cups broth or water drained from cooked
>   vegetables
> 1 tablespoon paprika
> Salt and pepper to taste

Brown meat in fat and proceed as in Basic Stew recipe. Add vegetables for last 5 minutes of simmering time. At serving time, return to boil and simmer 5 minutes; correct seasoning. Serves 6.

Note: If thickener is desired, add it at serving time when you correct the seasoning. Dissolve 2 tablespoons flour in 2 tablespoons cold water. While the pot is off the heating unit, stir flour mixture into the stew until lumps are absorbed. Return the pot to the heat and bring to a boil, stirring constantly. Cover, reduce heat, and simmer for several minutes.

Beef Bourguignon

SIMMERING TIME: 20 MINUTES
COOKER TIME: 3 TO 4 HOURS

10 to 12 boiling onions, peeled
3 cloves garlic, minced or pressed
3 tablespoons butter or bacon fat
2 pounds round steak, cut into 2-inch cubes
½ cup dried mushrooms, soaked, or 1 cup sliced fresh
    mushrooms
3 tablespoons flour
1 cup broth or water
1 cup red wine
6 potatoes, peeled and quartered lengthwise
½ teaspoon salt
¼ teaspoon pepper
1 tablespoon fresh or 1 teaspoon dried rosemary, thyme,
    or marjoram (if fresh, herbs should be well chopped)

In 3-quart pot, gently fry onions and garlic in butter until golden brown. Remove from pan. Brown meat and mushrooms in same pan, dust with flour, and stir liquids in gradually. Add onions, bring to boil, and cover. Reduce heat and simmer 20 minutes. Add potatoes and bring again to boil. Cover; reduce heat to simmer for 3 minutes more, and place in fireless cooker for 3 to 4 hours. At serving time, bring to boil and simmer 5 minutes; correct seasoning. Serves 6.

Note: If served with rice, omit potatoes and add flour to taste either at simmering time or just before serving. Three tablespoons of flour dissolved in about 3 tablespoons of cold water and beaten with a fork until smooth can be added for this purpose for the last 3 minutes of simmering time, or added and simmered for 3 minutes at serving time. A mixture of 2 teaspoons cornstarch in 2 tablespoons cold water may be substituted for a more transparent sauce. Use more cornstarch and water if you like a thick gravy.

Irish Stew

Perfected by our daughter Susan for her Irish husband.

SIMMERING TIME: 20 MINUTES
COOKER TIME: 3 HOURS

> 2 pounds lamb neck or shank, cut into 2-inch cubes
> 1 large onion, chopped

1 teaspoon caraway seeds (optional)
3 large potatoes, diced
6 large carrots, diced
1 stalk celery, cut into 1-inch diagonal pieces
½ head Savoy cabbage, about 1 pound, coarsely chopped
1 to 1½ cups water or broth, enough to fill pot two-thirds full
Salt and pepper to taste

In 6-quart pot, sauté meat, onion, and caraway seeds; proceed as for Basic Stew. Add vegetables for last 5 minutes of simmering time. At serving time, bring to boil and simmer 5 minutes; correct seasoning. Serves 6.

Curried Lamb

SIMMERING TIME: 15 TO 20 MINUTES
COOKER TIME: 2 TO 3 HOURS

2 pounds lamb, round steak or shoulder, cut into 1-inch cubes
2 tablespoons cooking fat
1 medium onion, chopped
1 clove garlic, minced or pressed
¼ cup dried mushrooms, soaked in hot or cold water for

2 hours, or ½ cup sliced fresh mushrooms
2 tablespoons flour
2 cups water or broth (some of the liquid may be beer or
   red wine)
1 teaspoon curry powder
½ teaspoon salt
1 bouquet garni, consisting of 1 stalk celery, 1 sprig
   parsley, 1 parsley root (if available), 1 carrot, 1 sprig
   rosemary, 1 sprig thyme, 1 sprig savory, or any other
   fresh or dried herbs to taste
1 tomato, quartered
1 teaspoon lemon juice

In skillet or frying pan, brown meat on all sides in fat; add onion, garlic, and mushrooms. Sprinkle flour over mixture and stir well. Remove from heat and stir in water; then transfer to a 2- to 3-quart pot and add curry, salt, bouquet garni, and tomato. Bring to boil, cover, reduce heat, and simmer for 15 to 20 minutes, depending on age and cut of lamb; place in fireless cooker for 2 to 3 hours. At serving time, bring to boil and simmer 5 minutes; discard bouquet garni and add lemon juice. Serve with rice. Serves 6.

Hungarian Beef Goulash

SIMMERING TIME: 20 MINUTES
COOKER TIME: 3 TO 4 HOURS

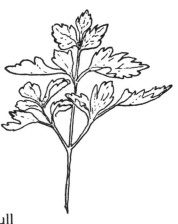

2 pounds beef chuck, cut into 1- or 2-inch cubes
2 large onions, sliced
2 cloves garlic, minced or pressed
1 teaspoon caraway seeds
1 tablespoon bacon fat
2 green peppers, cut into irregular 2-inch chunks
1 tablespoon tomato paste
4 tablespoons paprika
1 cup water or broth, or enough to fill pot two-thirds full
2 tablespoons flour
Salt and pepper to taste

In 3-quart pot, brown beef, onions, garlic, and caraway seeds in bacon fat. Proceed as for Basic Stew. Add peppers, tomato paste, and paprika together with water and flour for last 5 minutes of simmering time. Season with salt and pepper. At serving time, bring to boil and simmer 5 minutes; correct seasoning or thickening. Serve with Little Steamed Dumplings. Serves 6.

Note: If you cook for a Hungarian, add a small, hot chili pepper or a dash of cayenne.

Hungarian Pork Goulash

SIMMERING TIME: 15 MINUTES
COOKER TIME: 3 HOURS

2 pounds pork shoulder, cut into 1- or 2-inch cubes
2 onions, sliced
2 teaspoons caraway seeds
2 tablespoons cooking fat
2 mild green peppers, cut into 2-inch pieces
1 tablespoon tomato paste
4 tablespoons paprika
Dash of cayenne (optional)
2 tablespoons flour, for thickening
3 tablespoons sour cream, for garnish
Parsley or chives, chopped, for garnish

In 3-quart pot, brown pork, onions, and caraway seeds in cooking fat. Proceed as for Basic Stew. Add peppers, tomato paste, flour, and seasonings for last 5 minutes of simmering time. At serving time, bring to boil and simmer 5 minutes. Correct seasoning and thickening; garnish with sour cream and chopped parsley. Serves 6.

Variation: For Veal Goulash, substitute 2 pounds veal neck or shoulder for pork. This will require 2 hours' cooker time.

PAPRIKA: TRY IT, YOU'LL LIKE IT

The average cook on this side of the Atlantic, who has a 2-ounce container of paprika on the spice shelf and uses it only occasionally and sparingly, will be amazed (or appalled) when I add several tablespoons to a single recipe. But if you cook Hungarian, as I do, you use a lot of paprika. Purchase it by the pound at bulk rate (in specialty shops for spices) or you will go broke.

Over many years of cooking for and with my Hungarian husband, I have become convinced that paprika—particularly imported Hungarian paprika—is a wonderfully mild, savory condiment that gives a rich flavor and color to all appropriate recipes.

Szekely Goulash

SIMMERING TIME: 20 MINUTES
COOKER TIME: 3 TO 4 HOURS

1 large onion, chopped
2 cloves garlic, minced
2 tablespoons fat or rendered pork trimmings
2 tablespoons paprika
1 teaspoon caraway seeds
Pepper to taste
Cayenne to taste
1 quart fresh or canned sauerkraut
3 cups water (part sauerkraut juice, if desired)
2 pounds pork shoulder, cut into 1-inch cubes
2 tablespoons tomato purée or 4 medium tomatoes
2 tablespoons flour
1 cup sour cream, heavy sweet cream, or half-and-half

In 3-quart pot, sauté onion and garlic in fat. Remove from heat, add paprika, caraway seeds, pepper, and cayenne, and stir. Add sauerkraut, water, meat, and tomato purée; bring to boil. Cover, reduce heat, and simmer for 20 minutes. Place in fireless cooker for 3 to 4 hours. Before serving, stir flour into cold water, then add to gravy and simmer several minutes. Garnish with sour cream. Serves 6.

Paprika Chicken

SIMMERING TIME: 15 MINUTES
COOKER TIME: 2 HOURS

> 1 large onion, sliced
> 2 tablespoons chicken fat or other cooking fat
> 1 2- to 3-pound chicken with giblets, cut up
> 1 teaspoon caraway seeds (optional)
> 1 to 2 cups chicken broth or water
> 2 tablespoons paprika, or to taste
> 2 tablespoons vermouth or dry white wine (optional)
> 2 tablespoons cold water
> 2 tablespoons flour
> 3 tablespoons sour cream or yoghurt, for garnish

In 4-quart pot, brown onion in fat over medium heat. Add chicken pieces and caraway seeds, and brown briefly. Add broth, paprika, and vermouth; bring to boil. Cover and reduce heat; simmer 10 minutes. Remove from heat and stir in paste made from cold water and flour. Add green pepper and bring to boil. Cover; reduce heat and simmer for 5 minutes more. Place in fireless cooker for 2 hours. At serving time, bring to boil and simmer 5 minutes. Garnish with sour cream. Serves 6.

Note: Traditionally, this dish is served with small dumplings.

Boiled Tongue

SIMMERING TIME # 1: 30 MINUTES
COOKER TIME # 1: 3 TO 4 HOURS
SIMMERING TIME # 2: 10 MINUTES
COOKER TIME # 2: 3 TO 4 HOURS

1 2- to 3-pound fresh, pickled, or smoked tongue
Cold water, for soaking
1 bay leaf
8 peppercorns
1 parsley root, if available
1 teaspoon salt, only if using fresh tongue
Cold water, for cooking
½ cup vinegar or wine

If using smoked or pickled tongue, soak it in cold water for 2 hours or longer. Fresh tongue needs only careful scrubbing with brush. Place tongue, bay leaf, peppercorns, parsley root, and salt in 4-quart pot, and cover with cold water to within 2 inches of top. Bring to boil, cover, reduce heat, and simmer for 30 minutes. Place in fireless cooker for 3 to 4 hours or overnight. Take tongue out of water, remove skin and all remaining glands and fat, discard water, and return tongue to 4-quart pot. Cover with cold water and add vinegar. Bring to boil, cover, reduce heat, and simmer for 10 minutes. Return to fireless cooker for 3 to 4 hours. At serving time, slice meat into half-inch slices across grain of meat. Serve with Caper Sauce, Mustard Sauce, or prepared horseradish, or do as the Viennese do and serve with 2 teaspoons horseradish mixed with 1 cup applesauce. Tongue is also very good served cold. Serves 6 to 8.

Variation: Heart is prepared in almost the same way as tongue. Use a 2-pound whole heart or half of a very large beef heart, and soak it for several hours in cold water to which 2 tablespoons of vinegar have been added. Discard soaking water, cover with fresh cold water, and proceed as with tongue, using bay leaf, peppercorns, and salt, but not parsley root. After first cooker period, slice into half-inch slices, transfer to 3-quart pot, cover with Brown Onion Sauce, Tomato Sauce, or Mushroom Sauce, bring to boil, simmer for 10 minutes, place in fireless cooker for 2 to 3 hours, and serve with rice, noodles, or mashed potatoes. Serves 6.

Vegetables

Just as it's important to use good judgment when preparing fresh vegetables on a surface unit, it is important to do so when processing these delicate foods in the fireless cooker. Very tender, young garden vegetables such as spinach, peas, or very young, freshly picked green beans should be eaten raw or cooked only briefly. However, green beans harvested late in the season or left on the vine a little too long, or the new kind of sugarsnap peas, which require more cooking, can be prepared in the fireless cooker with brief simmering and cooker times and served with a sauce, or added to soups or stews during the last few minutes of simmering time.

Root vegetables such as carrots, beets, turnips, and celeriac do very well in the cooker, particularly if they are large or were harvested late in the season.

Green peppers, the outside stalks of celery, boiling onions, and shallots do well in the fireless cooker, boiled separately or added to other foods for the last few minutes of simmering time. Eggplant, which gets mushy when boiled, does not do well in a fireless cooker, but pumpkin, hubbard squash, spaghetti squash, and similar vegetables do very well. Young zucchini are too tender for the cooker, but large old ones—the ones you forgot to pick in time—or cucumbers that have suffered the same fate, also do well in the cooker.

When mixing vegetables, consider the cooking requirements of each one. If you're planning to cook carrots and peas together, for example, do the carrots in the cooker and add the peas 2 to 3 minutes before serving time.

Cooking requirements change according to the way the vegetable is cut. Tough old string beans will need to be cut into 1-inch sections or slivered. Large old carrots will do better sliced, but young vegetables can be cooked whole or with little cutting. Late in the season I often use a sauce to make vegetables attractive; tender young things need no embellishment or camouflage.

Artichokes

SIMMERING TIME: 10 MINUTES
COOKER TIME: 2 HOURS

3 medium artichokes
3 cloves garlic, peeled and halved
2 quarts water, or enough to fill 4-quart pot two-thirds full
1 teaspoon salt
Dip (below)

Cut off artichokes' stems and trim off sharp points of artichoke leaves with scissors. Tuck garlic between leaves. Place artichokes in pot with water, cover, and bring to boil. Reduce heat,

simmer for 10 minutes, and place in fireless cooker for 2 hours. At serving time, cut artichokes in half with sharp knife and remove inedible inner leaves—but not heart. Serve with dip, allowing half an artichoke per person. Serves 6.

DIP

> 3 tablespoons mayonnaise
> 3 tablespoons sour cream
> 2 teaspoons horseradish

Combine ingredients and serve cold.

Harvard Beets

SIMMERING TIME: 5 MINUTES
COOKER TIME: 2 HOURS

> 1½ pounds large beets, whole or cut depending on
> season
> 1 teaspoon caraway seeds
> 1 teaspoon salt
> 2 cups water
> 1 cup dry white wine or vinegar
> 3 tablespoons sugar
> 1½ tablespoons cornstarch, dissolved in cold water

Combine first four ingredients in 2-quart pot. Bring to boil, cover, reduce heat and simmer for 5 minutes. Place in fireless cooker for 2 hours. Ten minutes before serving time, lift beets out of water, peel, and cut into quarters or ¼-inch slices. Stir dissolved cornstarch into 1 cup liquid and correct seasoning. Simmer briefly, add beets, and reheat. Add wine and sugar last. Serves 6.

Red Cabbage

SIMMERING TIME: 10 MINUTES
COOKER TIME: 3 TO 4 HOURS

> 3 slices bacon or salt pork, diced
> 1 large onion, chopped
> 1 teaspoon caraway seeds
> 2 medium apples, grated
> 1 tablespoon sugar
> 2 pounds red cabbage, coarsely chopped or shredded
> 2 tablespoons flour
> 1 cup water or broth
> 3 tablespoons red wine or vinegar
> ¼ teaspoon pepper
> 1 teaspoon salt (omit if using broth)

In 3-quart pot, fry bacon with onion and caraway seeds until golden brown. Add grated apple and sugar, stir, and sauté for 2 to 3 minutes. Add chopped red cabbage, sprinkle flour over mixture, then add water and wine gradually and stir until flour is well blended. Bring to boil, cover, reduce heat, and simmer for 10 minutes. Place in fireless cooker for 3 to 4 hours. Serves 6.

Note: Traditionally this is served with roast goose, but it is a tasty and colorful accompaniment with sausage or meat.

Variation: This recipe is good for white or Savoy cabbage; use 2 sliced carrots in place of apple and sugar. (But don't use this for very tender young cabbage, which needs only minimal cooking or sautéeing.) Serve with sausage and dumplings or potatoes. Save leftover trunk of Savoy cabbage to cut into strips and serve raw as an appetizer.

Creamed Carrots

SIMMERING TIME: 5 MINUTES
COOKER TIME: 1 TO 2 HOURS

> 1½ pounds large carrots, halved lengthwise, then cut
>   diagonally into 2-inch sections
> 2 tablespoons butter or margarine
> 2 tablespoons flour

2 cups water or broth
Salt and pepper to taste
Parsley, chopped, for garnish

In 1½-quart pot, sauté carrots lightly in butter. Sprinkle flour over them and stir. Gradually add water, then add seasonings. Stir and bring to boil. Cover, reduce heat, simmer for 5 minutes, and place in fireless cooker for 1 to 2 hours. At serving time garnish with chopped parsley. Serves 6.

Potatoes in the Jacket

This daily staple, easy to cook in the fireless cooker, has a short cooker time and is therefore recommended for learning how to use the cooker. Even a single potato can be cooked in the fireless cooker, but be sure to use at least a 2-quart pot two-thirds full of water—small pots cool off too rapidly.

Cold water to fill pot two-thirds full
6 medium potatoes

Use either 3- or 4-quart pot, depending on size of potatoes (don't crowd them). Bring cold water and potatoes to boil together with lid on. Reduce heat and simmer for 5 minutes. Place in fireless cooker for 2 hours. Serves 6.

Note: Potatoes can be of different sizes and still get done evenly most of the time. (I reserve very large potatoes for use in other types of cooking.) When cooking new potatoes or recently harvested potatoes with very tender skins, it is best to simmer them only 1 to 2 minutes to avoid bursting or overcooking.

Mashed Potatoes

SIMMERING TIME: 1 TO 2 MINUTES
COOKER TIME: 2 HOURS

    6 medium potatoes, peeled and quartered
    Cold water to fill pot two-thirds full
    ½ cup lukewarm milk
    2 tablespoons butter, or to taste
    1 teaspoon salt
    Sliced and fried onion, for garnish

In 3- or 4-quart pot, depending on size of potatoes (don't crowd them), bring potatoes and cold water to boil. Reduce heat and simmer 1 to 2 minutes. Place in fireless cooker for 2 hours. At serving time drain, mash, stir in milk, butter, and salt, and serve garnished with onion. Serves 4 to 6.

Creamed Spinach, Viennese Style

I think this is a dish fit for the princess in a fairy tale, but I under-stand why cooks ordinarily shy away from preparing it—with regular cooking methods the sauce sticks to the bottom of the pan. But with the fireless cooker, there is no problem.

SIMMERING TIME: 1 MINUTE
COOKER TIME: 1 HOUR

1½ pounds spinach, washed, with stems removed
2 cups boiling water
3 tablespoons flour
2 tablespoons butter
2 cloves garlic, minced or pressed
1 small onion, chopped
2 tablespoons cream
¾ cup milk
½ teaspoon salt
½ teaspoon pepper
1 egg (optional)

Place spinach in bowl and pour boiling water over it; let it stand for a few minutes. In the meantime, brown flour in butter, add minced garlic and chopped onion, sauté briefly and remove from heat. Stir in cream, return to heat, and stir in milk slowly. Place in blender along with spinach, seasonings, and enough spinach water to allow blender to spin freely at medium speed until everything is mixed and reasonably smooth—2 to 3 minutes. Add egg last if used. Pour mixture into 1½-quart pot and gently bring to boil over medium heat, stirring to prevent sticking (about 2 to 3 minutes). Cover, reduce heat, and simmer for 1 minute. Place in fireless cooker for 1 hour. This is traditionally served with a fried egg gently resting on each serving— a feast for the eyes if you grew up in Vienna. Serves 6.

Winter Squash

All winter squash—hubbard squash, spaghetti squash, butternut squash, and others—can be prepared in the fireless cooker. Some need only very little cooking on the stove, and it may not be worthwhile to use the cooker; others require 40 minutes or more on the stove; all take 40 to 60 minutes if baked, depending on the variety. I consider it worthwhile to cook a whole squash or pumpkin at one time, using part of it the same day as a vegetable course or to make a pie, and freezing the rest.

SIMMERING TIME: 5 MINUTES
COOKER TIME: 1 TO 2 HOURS

1 medium winter squash, about 2 to 3 pounds
Boiling salted water to fill 3-quart pot two-thirds full
2 tablespoons brown sugar
2 tablespoons butter
Salt and pepper to taste
Parsley, chopped, for garnish (optional)

With large, strong knife cut unpeeled squash into long strips about 1 to 2 inches wide. Put them into boiling water and cover. Reduce heat and simmer for 5 minutes. Place in fireless cooker for 1 to 2 hours. At serving time, drain, peel, and put 2 cups of squash into 1-quart saucepan over medium heat. Add brown sugar and butter, and stir with wire whisk or fork until smooth, about 2 to 3 minutes. Season, garnish with chopped parsley if desired, and serve promptly before it sticks to the pan. For freezing, remainder of squash should be drained well, peeled, cut into 1- to 2-inch cubes, packed in pint-size freezer bags (suck out air with drinking straw), and sealed with wire twist. Serves 6 generously.

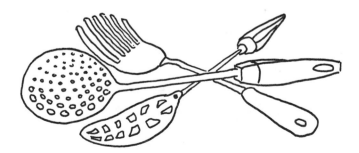

Salads

There are many delicious vegetable salads that involve some cooking, but I have included here only those that require long cooking periods for the vegetables used. For these the fireless cooker is a great time- and energy-saver; for vegetables requiring only brief cooking on the stove (fresh peas, for example), the fireless cooker is not useful and I have not included recipes for them.

A combination of leftover hot potato salad, lentil salad, and bean salad (recipes follow) makes a very good mixed salad, served cold. The mixture cannot be prepared together because the preparation and cooker times are too different.

Chilled Green Bean Salad

SIMMERING TIME: 5 MINUTES
COOKER TIME: 2 HOURS

    3 cups lightly salted boiling water
    2 pounds green beans, cut into 2-inch pieces
    1 small onion, chopped
    2 tablespoons diced, fried bacon (optional)

Vinaigrette Dressing (following recipe)
Salt and pepper to taste

In 1½-quart pot, add beans to boiling water and bring again to boil. Cover, reduce heat, simmer for 5 minutes, and place in fireless cooker for 2 hours. Drain, add remaining ingredients, and refrigerate. Toss and adjust seasoning before serving. (This salad is also good served hot, and can be successfully reheated or kept hot in cooker.) Serves 6.

Note: If you have very young tender beans, fresh from the garden, it is not practical to process them in the cooker. Five to 7 minutes of boiling will make them tender enough. But the cooker is useful if the beans are harvested late or kept in storage and therefore require longer cooking periods.

Vinaigrette Dressing

4 tablespoons olive oil
2 tablespoons vinegar
¼ teaspoon salt
¼ teaspoon pepper
¼ teaspoon dry mustard dissolved in 1 tablespoon
    cold water

1 tablespoon (combined) fresh oregano, fennel, thyme,
   or other herbs, finely chopped, or 1 teaspoon
   dried herbs

Put all ingredients into jar and shake well before pouring over salad just before serving. Lemon juice may be substituted for some or all of vinegar. Toss salad with dressing and store left-over dressing in refrigerator. Serves 6.

Celeriac Salad

SIMMERING TIME: 5 MINUTES
COOKER TIME: 4 HOURS

1 medium celeriac (celery root), trimmed, scrubbed,
   and halved lengthwise
1½ quarts cold water, or to 2 inches from top of pot
Vinaigrette Dressing
Chopped parsley
Paprika, for garnish

In 3½-quart pot, bring celeriac to boiling in cold water. Reduce heat and simmer for 5 minutes. Place in fireless cooker for 4 hours. Drain, cool, and peel, then cut into thin slices and toss gently with dressing. Garnish with parsley and paprika, refrigerate, and serve cold. Serves 6.

Note: Save the water the celeriac was cooked in. It adds particularly good flavor to soups. Also, whenever I can, I add celeriac to boiled beef for the last 5 minutes of simmering time; then at serving time I remove the celeriac to cool and be served as a salad with the same meal or later.

Hot Potato Salad

SIMMERING TIME: 5 MINUTES
COOKER TIME: 2 HOURS

2 pounds or 7 to 8 medium potatoes
Cold water, to fill pot two-thirds full
6 tablespoons vinegar
6 tablespoons cooking oil
1 large onion, chopped
2 slices bacon, diced and fried
1 teaspoon mustard
3 tablespoons chopped dill pickles
Chopped parsley or chives
A sprinkle of paprika
Salt and pepper to taste

Put potatoes and cold water into a 4½-quart pot, bring to boil, reduce heat, and simmer for 5 minutes. Place in fireless cooker for 2 hours. Drain, peel, and slice potatoes, and return them to

115

pot in which they were cooked. Mix all other ingredients in separate bowl, then add them to potatoes and serve while still hot. (If you want to keep this salad hot for up to 30 minutes, cover and return pot to cooker. Trying to reheat it spoils its appearance and flavor, so once this has cooled off, it's better served cold.) Serves 6.

Variation: Make Cold Potato Salad by substituting mayonnaise for vinegar-and-oil dressing, and garnish with 3 sliced hard-cooked eggs.

Beet Salad

SIMMERING TIME: 5 MINUTES
COOKER TIME: 3 HOURS

> 1½ quarts lightly salted water
> 2 pounds fresh beets
> Vinaigrette Dressing
> 1 teaspoon caraway seeds

In 3½-quart pot, bring water and beets to boil; water level should be about 2 inches from top of pot, but need not entirely cover beets. Cover, reduce heat, and simmer for 5 minutes. Place in fireless cooker for 3 hours. Chill; at serving time, peel and slice beets and serve with Vinaigrette Dressing and caraway seeds. Serves 6.

Note: Very large beets, particularly late in the season, may need 7 to 10 minutes of simmering time; small young beets, early in the season, may need less than 5 minutes, but will not be noticeably overcooked if given 5 minutes.

Dried Bean Salad

Various types of beans require different cooking times; in addition, various types of processing change the required cooking times. Check the information on the package label. The instructions given here are for long-cooking beans, beans that need 3 hours or more of stove-top cooking. If the label suggests shorter cooking periods, reduce the simmering time to 10 minutes and use about 1 cup less water.

SIMMERING TIME: 15 MINUTES
COOKER TIME: 3 TO 4 HOURS

> 1 cup dried beans
> 1 quart lightly salted cold water
> Vinaigrette Dressing
> Chopped parsley

A sprinkle of paprika
2 slices bacon, diced and fried (optional)

To prepare beans for cooking, see my introduction to the section on Legumes. After soaking, bring beans to boil in water they were soaking in. Cover, reduce heat, simmer for 15 minutes, and place in fireless cooker for 3 to 4 hours. Drain, cool, and toss salad with Vinaigrette Dressing. Garnish with parsley and paprika. Fried bacon bits sprinkled over salad at serving time make it dressier. Serves 6.

Note: Most beans will be tender after the treatment suggested above. Soy beans or, very occasionally, other extra-tough beans will require a second simmering time of 10 to 15 minutes and a second cooker time of 4 to 5 hours.

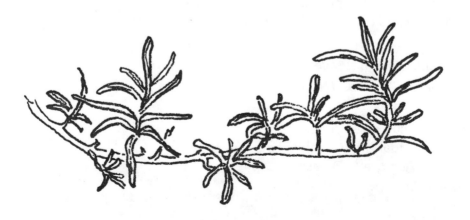

Sauces

The fireless cooker is ideal for cream sauces because they require long cooking times and constant stirring when cooked over fire to prevent them from burning and to help their ingredients blend without lumping.

The basic Cream Sauce recipe can be varied in dozens of different ways with fresh or cooked vegetables, fresh or cooked meats, herbs, condiments, pickles, capers, and so on. It is the ingenious use of a sauce that turns humble leftovers into a gourmet's delight.

Uncooked foods are added to the sauce after being sautéed in hot butter or fat. Chopped or sliced onions, garlic, herbs, sliced or diced celery, and similar vegetables retain their shape and flavor better this way. Uncooked meat is browned in the fat before the flour is added.

Cooked or otherwise processed foods—for example, leftover boiled or roasted meat, cooked vegetables, and capers, anchovies, or mustard—are best added last, when the Cream Sauce is almost finished, and all ingredients, including the liquid, should be brought to the boiling point together.

Cream Sauce

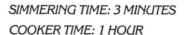

5 tablespoons shortening or any other cooking fat
5 tablespoons flour
2 cups water, broth, milk, or liquid from cooking
    vegetables
Seasonings and garnishes to taste

In 1-quart pot, melt shortening, add flour, and brown lightly while stirring over medium heat for about 3 minutes. Remove from heat and slowly add some of liquid, stirring constantly to avoid lumps. Return to heat, bring to boil, add remaining liquid, season, cover, reduce heat, and simmer for 3 minutes. Place in fireless cooker for 1 hour. Makes 2 cups.

Variation: To make Caper Sauce, prepare Cream Sauce in 1½-quart pot, using broth or fish stock as liquid. At serving time add 3 tablespoons of drained, chopped capers, and garnish with parsley. This sauce is particularly good with fish, and will eliminate the fishy taste of frozen fish. For spicier sauce, add 2 tablespoons of caper brine at serving time.

Brown Onion Sauce

SIMMERING TIME: 3 MINUTES

COOKER TIME: 1 HOUR

5 tablespoons fat
2 medium onions, chopped, or equivalent amount of
   shallots
2 tablespoons sugar
1 teaspoon caraway seeds
5 tablespoons flour
2 cups broth or water
1 tablespoon vinegar
1 teaspoon lemon juice (optional)
Salt and pepper to taste
Parsley, chopped, for garnish

In skillet, heat fat, add onions, and sauté till light brown. Add sugar and caraway seeds, and stir over medium heat until dark golden brown. Add flour and brown until dark brown. Remove from heat and add 1 cup broth, stirring constantly to avoid lumps. When sauce is smooth, transfer it to 1-quart pot, add remaining broth, plus vinegar and lemon juice, and bring to boil. Cover, reduce heat to simmer for 3 minutes, and place in fireless cooker for 1 hour. Correct seasoning, garnish, and serve. Makes 2 cups.

Note: The start in the frying pan is suggested because many enameled pots will suffer from scraping over relatively high heat during the browning process. If you are using a stainless steel pot with a sturdy bottom, the entire procedure can be done in one pot, saving the trouble of the transfer.

Variation #1: Leftover cooked meat may be added at simmering time, or meat may be heated in sauce just before serving. Serve over rice or noodles, or with hash brown potatoes. Accompanied by a salad, it makes a fast and inexpensive dinner.

Variation #2: To make White Onion Sauce, eliminate sugar and browning.

Tomato Sauce

SIMMERING TIME: 3 MINUTES
COOKER TIME: 1 HOUR

> 5 tablespoons fat
> 1 teaspoon caraway seeds
> 2 tablespoons sugar
> 5 tablespoons flour
> 1 cup broth or water

1 pound fresh tomatoes, quartered
Salt and pepper to taste
Parsley or chives, chopped

In 1½-quart pot, melt fat, add caraway seeds, sugar, and flour, and brown lightly over medium heat. Remove from heat and add broth slowly, stirring constantly. Add tomatoes, cover, and bring to boil. Reduce heat and simmer for 3 minutes. Place in fireless cooker for 1 hour. Season, put through sieve or blender, and garnish with chopped parsley before serving. Makes 2 cups.

Mushroom Sauce

SIMMERING TIME: 3 MINUTES
COOKER TIME: 1 HOUR

1 pound fresh mushrooms, sliced
5 tablespoons butter
5 tablespoons flour
2 cups water, skim milk, or broth
Parsley or chives, chopped

In 1-quart pot, lightly sauté sliced mushrooms in butter for about 2 to 3 minutes. Sprinkle flour over mixture and stir. Proceed as with Cream Sauce. Makes 2 cups.

Variation #1: One medium onion, chopped, may be sautéed with mushrooms, and 2 tablespoons of sour cream or dry white wine may be added at serving time. If you are well trained and experienced in gathering wild mushrooms, chanterelles are particularly good in this sauce. Choose young, firm specimens and garnish with fresh chopped basil.

Variation #2: To make Mushroom Sauce with dried mushrooms, follow Mushroom Sauce recipe, using 1 cup dried mushrooms washed several times in cold water, soaked in hot water for 20 minutes then drained and chopped.

Mustard Sauce

2 cups Cream Sauce
1 tablespoon mustard
1 tablespoon lemon juice
Salt and pepper to taste
2 eggs, hard-cooked and sliced
A sprinkle of paprika, for garnish

Prepare Cream Sauce recipe in 1-quart pot. At serving time season with mustard, lemon juice, and salt and pepper. Add eggs and garnish with paprika. This sauce is particularly good served with fish. Makes 2 cups.

Spaghetti Sauce

SIMMERING TIME: 10 MINUTES
COOKER TIME: 1 TO 2 HOURS

    1 pound lean ground beef
    1 medium onion, chopped
    1 clove garlic, minced
    1 teaspoon fresh oregano, chopped
    1 teaspoon fresh basil, chopped
    1 teaspoon fresh thyme, chopped
    Salt and pepper to taste
    4 large tomatoes, diced, or 2 6-ounce cans tomato sauce
    2 tablespoons flour stirred with 2 tablespoons cold water
      (optional)

Crumble ground beef into skillet and brown lightly; remove excess fat with spoon. Add onion, garlic, herbs, and seasonings, and gently heat mixture for 2 or 3 minutes. Add tomatoes, transfer to 2-quart pot, and bring to boil. Cover, reduce heat, simmer for 10 minutes, and place in fireless cooker for 1 to 2 hours. At serving time, bring to boil and simmer 5 minutes. If sauce needs thickening, add flour and cold water at serving time or just before simmering time. Serves 6.

Dumplings

Dumpling in a Napkin

SIMMERING TIME: 5 MINUTES
COOKER TIME: 2 TO 3 HOURS

4 quarts boiling water, salted
3 cups unseasoned bread stuffing, cubed or crumbled
1 cup milk
1 large onion, chopped
3 tablespoons butter or cooking fat
1 clove garlic, minced
2 tablespoons fresh rosemary, thyme, or other herbs,
    finely chopped, or 2 teaspoons dried herbs
3 tablespoons flour
2 teaspoons salt
3 eggs, beaten
Parsley, chopped, for garnish

In 6-quart pot, bring salted water to boil. In the meantime soak
bread stuffing in milk, stirring occasionally. Gently fry chopped
onion in butter until golden brown; add garlic and herbs and
sauté briefly. Combine stuffing and milk, onion mixture, flour,
and salt in large bowl; add eggs last and stir until well mixed, so

all the bread is well moistened and comes together to form a doughlike mass. Place large old napkin or double layer of cheesecloth measuring 14 by 14 inches in another bowl, add dough, and tie corners crosswise, making a large, ball-shaped dumpling. Place gently into boiling water, bring again to boil, cover, reduce heat, and simmer for 5 minutes. Place pot in fireless cooker for 2 to 3 hours. At serving time lift dumpling out of hot water and drain in colander. Remove napkin and slice dumpling into even half-inch slices. Garnish with parsley and serve promptly with salad to make a simple, meatless supper. Or serve with stew and gravy. Serves 6.

Note: Leftover dumpling is particularly good when cut into bite-size pieces and fried gently in butter until golden brown, with or without a beaten egg stirred in just before serving.

Variation: Divide dough to make 12 round dumplings about 1½ inches in diameter. Prepare something for center of each—fried onions or bits of ham, Swiss cheese, vegetables, or fried bacon. In 4-quart pot boil 2 quarts water to which 1 teaspoon salt has been added and gently put in a few dumplings at a time so water will continue to simmer. When all are in, cover, reduce heat, and simmer for 1 minute. Place in cooker for 2 to 3 hours. Garnish with chopped parsley and serve with any meat-and-gravy dish.

Potato Dumplings

SIMMERING TIME: 1 TO 2 MINUTES
COOKER TIME: 2 HOURS

6 medium potatoes, peeled, cooked in fireless cooker,
   and grated while warm
¾ to 1 cup flour
2 tablespoons regular Cream of Wheat
2 tablespoons butter
1 egg
1 teaspoon salt
Fried, diced bacon or fried, sliced onion
Boiling water, to fill 4-quart pot half full

Combine grated potatoes with flour, Cream of Wheat, butter, egg, and salt; knead together to make reasonably smooth dough. Roll out to half-inch thickness and, using floured knife or pastry wheel, cut into 2-by-2-inch diamonds. Place pieces of bacon or onion in center of diamonds, fold corners over filling, and roll into dumpling shape. Drop dumplings into 4-quart pot half full of boiling water. Bring again to boil, simmer a minute or 2, and place in fireless cooker for 2 hours. Serves 6.

Note: This recipe is a childhood memory, and the element of surprise never lost its appeal, even if in tough times the filling was discovered to be only a fried bread cube.

Variation: Substitute cherries or raisins for filling, and serve as dessert.

Cream of Wheat Dumplings

This is a good recipe to make with young children. They love to roll dumplings.

SIMMERING TIME: 1 MINUTE
COOKER TIME: ½ TO 1 HOUR

> 2 tablespoons butter or margarine
> 1 cup milk
> ¾ cup regular Cream of Wheat
> 1 egg
> 2 quarts broth

In small pan heat butter, add milk, and bring to brief boil over medium heat. Remove pan from heating unit and stir in Cream of Wheat. Return pan to low heat and continue stirring until mixture comes away from bottom of pan, about 30 seconds. Cool, and stir in egg. Shape dough into 1½-inch balls, slightly moistening hands to keep dough from sticking. In the meantime bring broth to boil in 3-quart pot, and drop dumplings in, about 5 or 6 at a time, to allow broth to continue boiling gently. Cover, and simmer for 1 minute, then place in fireless cooker for 30 minutes to 1 hour. (These can be cooked very easily without the fireless cooker—they take about 15 to 20 minutes simmering on low heat—but they get especially nice and plump in the cooker without falling apart, which happens easily if they are boiled too hard or too long on a surface unit.) Serves 6.

Variation #1: Serve with broth or soup, garnished with chopped parsley.

Variation #2: Drain dumplings and serve with stew and gravy.

Variation #3: For a vegetarian supper, serve dumplings with Mushroom Sauce and salad.

Variation #4: To serve as dessert, use lightly salted water instead of broth, and serve with fruit or syrup.

Cottage Cheese Dumplings

SIMMERING TIME: 1 MINUTE
COOKER TIME: 1 HOUR

¼ cup butter or margarine
1 pound cottage cheese, passed through sieve or
   whirled in blender
3 eggs

1 cup plus 2 tablespoons regular Cream of Wheat
2 tablespoons flour
¾ cup bread crumbs
1½ quarts lightly salted boiling water
3 tablespoons butter, unsalted if available, melted

Beat butter until fluffy, about 3 to 4 minutes. Add cottage cheese, eggs, Cream of Wheat, flour, and about half of bread crumbs. Stir until blended. Shape into 2-inch dumplings and drop into gently boiling salted water, 2 or 3 at a time, to maintain a gentle boil. Cover and continue boiling for 1 minute. Place in fireless cooker for 1 hour. Meanwhile, sauté remaining bread crumbs in butter; set aside. Drain dumplings, roll in sautéed bread crumbs, and serve hot. Makes 12 dumplings and serves 4 to 6.

Variation: To serve as dessert, omit butter-bread-crumb garnish and serve with canned fruit.

Little Steamed Dumplings

In Austria, these are called *Nockerl.* I don't recommend cooking them in the fireless cooker because they only take about 10 minutes on a stove top. However, I include the recipe here because these are traditionally served with all kinds of goulash and several other foods in this book.

2 quarts water
1 teaspoon salt
3 ¼ cups sifted flour
¼ cup butter or shortening, melted
1 cup milk
2 eggs
1 ½ teaspoons salt

In 4-quart pot, bring water and salt to boil. In the meantime, place flour in large bowl and make hollow in middle.

Beat milk and eggs together and pour mixture into hollow, stirring in gradually with a fork. Add melted butter last and beat vigorously for a few minutes, until all flour is worked in and dough is fairly firm and reasonably smooth. (If a strong and willing helper is available, I happily turn this job over to him or her. Some of the more modern mixing machines in your kitchen may do it; mine does not.) With tablespoon, drop 2-inch balls of dough into boiling water; keep spoon wet to prevent dough from sticking. Cover and simmer about 10 minutes or until dumplings are plump and float to top of water. Serves 6.

Note: Leftover dumplings are particularly good warmed over in butter in a covered frying pan over medium heat until golden brown. Just before serving, remove the pan from the heat and stir in a beaten egg. Sprinkle chopped parsley over them and serve with salad for a delicious lunch.

Steamed Foods: Breads, Souffles, and Puddings

The fireless cooker, in combination with a tube mold, can be used to make delicious breads and soufflés as well as puddings or foods whose recipes start, "In the top of a double boiler . . ."

It's necessary to have a tubed mold with a tight lid; mine is a 1-quart mold whose central tube extends almost to the level of the lid. The smooth, fluted sides of the mold, flaring slightly toward the top, make unmolding the finished food very easy.

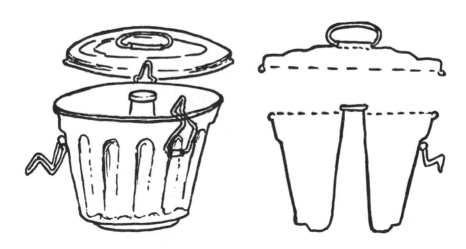

Grease the mold and the lid well, and sprinkle all inside surfaces with bread crumbs or flour to facilitate the unmolding. (For puddings, substitute sugar for the bread crumbs.) Be sure to leave at least 2 inches of headspace when pouring batters into the mold; this allows for expansion during cooking.

While you are mixing the batter, bring a quart of water to boiling in a 6-quart pot. After you have poured the batter into the mold and secured its lid, place the mold in the center of the pot, cover the pot, and quickly return the water to an active boil so that you can see the steam emerging from under the lid. Reduce the heat to maintain steaming (little curls of steam will continue to escape), and start the simmering time.

Steamed Whole Wheat Bread

I owe this recipe to a group of women in South Africa who call themselves Women for Peace. I received their pamphlet (see Bibliography) and adapted this recipe for my own kitchen.

SIMMERING (STEAMING) TIME: 30 MINUTES
COOKER TIME: 3 HOURS OR MORE

> 1 cake fresh yeast or 1 tablespoon dry yeast
> ½ teaspoon sugar
> 1¼ cups warm water
> 3 cups whole wheat flour
> ½ teaspoon salt
> 5 cups boiling water, for steaming

Mix yeast with sugar, then with ¼ cup warm water. Put flour in large bowl, make hollow in middle, and pour yeast mixture into it. Sprinkle a little flour over yeast and let sit 15 minutes, then mix yeast with flour. Gradually add remaining cup of warm water and knead until all the flour is worked in and dough no longer sticks to your hands, about 5 to 7 minutes. Put dough into oiled 2-quart pot, cover, and place in fireless cooker to rise until doubled in bulk—about 2 hours. Knead dough again, and return to cooker for second rising of 20 to 30 minutes. Cover pot, place in center of another pot large enough to hold it for

135

steaming (I use a 6-quart pot), and pour 5 cups boiling water into larger pot. Bring water back to boiling, cover larger pot, reduce heat, and steam 30 minues. Place large pot containing small pot in fireless cooker for 3 hours or more. The resulting bread is pale and has no crust, but is a very tasty, dense, peasant-style bread, similar in every way to oven-baked bread made entirely from whole wheat flour.

If you want to add color and crust to the loaf, brush with milk, then place under broiler for a few minutes. You can get the same result by brushing with oil and holding over cooking unit or campfire. You can also substitute all-purpose white flour or a mixture of flours for whole wheat flour. Be sure to allow for minor differences in rising time and size of container. Makes 1 loaf.

Note: Any bowl made of material that can stand heat and has a pleasing shape for making bread can be used if securely covered with foil.

Boston Steamed Brown Bread

This method is used by Women for Peace, in South Africa.

SIMMERING (STEAMING) TIME: 30 MINUTES
COOKER TIME: SEVERAL HOURS OR OVERNIGHT

Butter, for greasing mold
½ cup graham flour
½ cup whole wheat flour
½ cup yellow cornmeal
½ teaspoon salt
1 teaspoon baking soda
1 cup buttermilk
6 tablespoons molasses or corn syrup
½ cup chopped raisins
5 cups boiling water, for steaming

Have all ingredients at room temperature. Thoroughly grease 1-quart tube mold and its tight-fitting lid with butter. Bring water to boil in 6-quart pot. In the meantime, combine dry ingredients in one bowl, and stir buttermilk and molasses together in another. Mix liquids with dry ingredients and stir until batter is smooth. Add raisins to batter, pour batter into mold, and securely fasten lid. Place mold in center of pot with boiling water, cover, and return water to boiling. Reduce heat, and steam for 30 minutes. Place large pot containing mold in fireless cooker for several hours or overnight. At serving time, loosen bread from sides and stem of mold at upper edge only, then turn out onto plate or cutting board. Slice and serve warm or cold. Serves 6.

Steamed Dinner Rolls

SIMMERING (STEAMING) TIME: 30 MINUTES
COOKER TIME: 3 HOURS OR MORE

2 ¾ cups all-purpose flour
1 cake fresh yeast or 1 tablespoon dry yeast
½ teaspoon sugar
1 ¼ cups warm water or milk
2 to 3 tablespoons butter, softened, for buttering pot and
    dough
5 cups boiling water, for steaming
Milk, beaten egg yolk, or melted butter, for browning rolls

Place flour in large bowl and make well in middle. Stir yeast
and sugar together, then add ¼ cup warm water and stir until
smooth. Pour yeast mixture into well and sprinkle a little flour
over it to make "sponge." Let sit 15 minutes, then stir flour and
yeast together. Gradually add remaining cup of warm water.
When dough comes together, knead with your hands until all
flour is worked in and dough no longer sticks to your hands
—about 5 to 7 minutes. Warm small pot (mine holds 2 quarts
and measures 3½ inches high and 7½ inches across, with a
tight-fitting lid) briefly in oven or for 10 seconds on unit set at
medium heat. Put dough in pot, cover, and put into fireless
cooker to rise until doubled in size, about 1 to 1½ hours. Knead
dough again for 3 to 4 minutes, then divide into 10 or 12 ball-

shaped pieces. Butter inside of small pot and brush sides of dough balls with butter as you place them side by side in pot. Cover and put in warm place or in fireless cooker again to rise for another 20 to 30 minutes. Place small pot in center of pot large enough to hold it for steaming, with lid properly closed (mine has a 6-quart capacity and measures 4½ inches high and 11½ inches across). Pour 5 cups boiling water into larger pot, and return to boiling. Cover larger pot, reduce heat, and steam for 30 minutes, then place large pot containing small pot in fireless cooker for 3 hours or more. When you turn dinner rolls out of pot, they will be completely cooked but will have no crust. Brush with milk, egg yolk, or melted butter, and place under broiler for a few minutes to produce good color and crust. (Oiling or buttering the tops and suspending the whole group of dinner rolls upside down over a heating unit on medium heat will also work. I use the steel ring from my wok and put broiler rack across it about 2 inches above the stove-top heating unit to accomplish this. The rolls brown in 4 minutes.) Makes 10 to 12 rolls.

Cheese Soufflé

SIMMERING TIME: 10 MINUTES
COOKER TIME: 2 TO 3 HOURS

Melted butter, for greasing mold
Flour, for dusting mold

3 tablespoons butter
3 tablespoons sifted flour
¾ cup milk
¼ teaspoon paprika
¼ teaspoon pepper
¼ pound Swiss cheese or cheddar, grated
3 egg yolks and 4 egg whites
1 quart boiling water, for steaming

Butter tubed 1-quart pudding form with tight-fitting lid, coating inside of form and lid and central tube, then dust inside with flour. In 1½-quart pot, melt butter, add flour, and stir over medium heat until blended and bubbling. Remove from heat and gradually add milk, stirring constantly. Return mixture to heat for 2 to 3 minutes to let thicken; add seasonings and cheese, stirring constantly until blended; set aside to cool. Beat egg whites until stiff but not dry; set aside. Bring water to active boiling in 6-quart pot (you may use 4- or 5-quart pot if it is tall enough to accommodate pudding form and allow proper closing of lid). Add egg yolks to cooled cheese mixture, then fold in beaten egg whites and pour batter into buttered and floured pudding form, which should be only three-quarters full or have about 2 inches headspace to allow soufflé to rise. Cover and lock lid on pudding mold and place in center of pot in which water is now actively boiling. Cover, return water to boiling, then reduce heat, and steam for 10 minutes. Place pot containing pudding form in cooker for 2 to 3 hours. At serving time loosen soufflé around wall and tube of pudding form, then place heated plate over top and invert to unmold. Serves 4 to 6.

Spinach Soufflé

SIMMERING TIME: 10 MINUTES
COOKER TIME: 2 HOURS

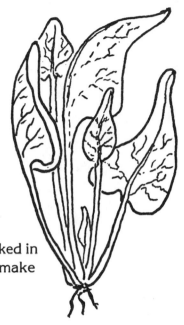

Butter, for greasing mold
1 tablespoon bread crumbs
1 small onion, chopped
1 clove garlic, minced
3 tablespoons butter
3 tablespoons flour
¾ cup cream or broth
1 pound spinach, stems removed or chopped, soaked in
    boiling water for 2 to 3 minutes, and drained to make
    1 cup
½ teaspoon salt
¼ teaspoon pepper
3 eggs, separated
1 quart boiling water, for steaming

Evenly butter tubed, 1-quart pudding mold 5 inches high and 6½ inches across, plus its tight-fitting lid; sprinkle bread crumbs all over inside. Sauté onion and garlic in butter in skillet for 1 to 2 minutes; add flour and stir. Remove from heat and slowly add cream, stirring constantly. Place mixture in blender along with spinach and seasonings. Whirl at medium speed 2 or 3 minutes, or until smooth. Add egg yolks and

141

briefly whirl at low speed until mixed, about 30 seconds. In a separate bowl, beat egg whites until stiff. In the meantime bring water to active boil in 6-quart pot. Fold egg whites into spinach mixture gently and pour into greased and crumbed mold. Close lid, secure locks, and place mold into steaming water. Return water to boiling, cover, reduce heat, and steam for 10 minutes. Place pot containing pudding mold in fireless cooker for 2 hours. At serving time, use pointed knife to loosen edges of soufflé from walls and tube. Place plate over top of mold and turn upside down to unmold. Serve with creamed Mushroom Sauce. Serves 6.

Variation: Substitute 1 cup of cooked, chopped carrots, broccoli, cauliflower, or other vegetables for the spinach.

Rice and Apple Pudding

SIMMERING TIME: 15 MINUTES
COOKER TIME: 3 HOURS

2 tablespoons butter, for greasing mold
2 tablespoons bread crumbs, for coating mold
1½ cups milk
2 cups cooked rice
3 eggs, separated

3 tablespoons sugar
2 tablespoons butter
½ teaspoon salt
⅓ cup raisins
¼ cup chopped nuts
1 apple, diced
1 quart water

Butter 1-quart pudding mold and lid; coat with bread crumbs and set aside. Combine egg yolks, sugar, butter, and salt; beat until smooth, about 2 or 3 minutes. Add raisins, apple, and nuts. Combine cooked rice with egg-yolk mixture. Beat egg whites until stiff, then fold into rest of ingredients and pour batter into buttered and crumbed pudding mold. Close and lock lid. In the meantime, heat water to boiling in 6-quart pot. Place pudding mold in center of pot, cover, and steam for 10 minutes. Place in cooker for 3 hours. Loosen edges with knife and unmold. Serve hot or cold with any fruit syrup, fresh or frozen berries, or any other colorful fruit topping. Serves 6.

Note: If necessary, the top of a 3-quart double boiler can be buttered and crumbed and filled with the batter as above, and steamed over the bottom of the double boiler for 10 minutes; then the whole unit—bottom, top, and lid—may be placed in the cooker for 1 to 2 hours.

Cottage Cheese Pudding

SIMMERING TIME: 15 MINUTES
COOKER TIME: 3 HOURS

3 tablespoons butter
1 cup cottage cheese, passed through sieve or swirled
 in blender until smooth
3 eggs, separated
½ cup sugar
½ cup or more slivered almonds
¼ cup or more raisins
½ teaspoon almond extract (optional)
Butter, for greasing mold
1 tablespoon sugar
1 quart water

In blender, swirl butter until fluffy, about 10 or 15 seconds. Add cottage cheese and swirl 10 seconds more, add egg yolks and sugar, and blend briefly until mixture looks uniformly yellow. Scrape out of blender with rubber spatula into large bowl and add almonds, raisins, and almond extract. In a different bowl, beat egg whites until stiff but not dry. Stir about a quarter of egg whites into cottage cheese mixture, then fold in the rest. Pour this mixture into pudding mold that has been buttered and dusted with sugar. Cover, place closed pudding mold in center of 4- to 6-quart pot in which water has been brought to boiling.

Return water to active boil, cover pot, reduce heat, and steam for 15 minutes. Place in fireless cooker for 3 hours. At serving time, open pudding mold and loosen pudding from sides and central stem with pointed knife.

Turn pudding out of mold by placing plate over top and turning mold upside down onto it. Serve warm with raspberry syrup or fresh raspberries or strawberries. (Any canned fruit can be substituted in winter. The more colorful the better.) Serves 6 to 8.

Caramel Custard

This custard can be made in any pot or casserole that holds about 1½ quarts and fits inside one of your large pots while allowing the lid of the larger one to close. A souffle dish with foil tied over the top can also be used for the smaller container. A 3-quart double boiler that fits into your cooker will work well, too, but if you use a glass container be sure to warm it carefully before pouring in the hot caramel or it may crack.

SIMMERING TIME: 10 MINUTES
COOKER TIME: 1 TO 2 HOURS

> 1 cup milk
> 1 tablespoon sugar
> 6 eggs
> ½ cup sugar, for caramel
> ½ teaspoon grated nutmeg
> 1 quart water, for steaming

Combine milk, 1 tablespoon sugar, and eggs in bowl and mix until well blended; a wire whisk is best for this job. In small pan with sturdy bottom (iron is best), heat remaining sugar first over high heat for 2 to 3 minutes, then over medium heat until melted and golden yellow, stirring gently with fork. It will be lumpy for a while, but lumps will dissolve gradually after 5 to 7 minutes of stirring. When all sugar is liquid, pour quickly into your pudding mold or small pot and tilt container in all directions to make it coat the wall about 2 inches up the side. Pour in custard mixture, sprinkle nutmeg over top, and cover with lid or foil. Place inside larger pot, in which you have brought water to active boil. Cover, reduce heat, and simmer for 10 minutes.

Place in cooker for 1 to 2 hours. Serve hot or cold with caramel sauce from bottom of pan poured over each helping. Serves 6.

Note: If using a double boiler, fill the bottom unit with 2 cups of water and fill the top with ingredients according to the recipe. Put the entire assembled double boiler into the cooker.

Steamed Nutcake

SIMMERING TIME: 15 MINUTES
COOKER TIME: 3 TO 4 HOURS

2 teaspoons cooking oil
2 teaspoons sugar
4½ ounces shelled walnuts (equals about 1⅓ cups)
⅔ cup sugar
4 egg yolks
1 teaspoon grated baking chocolate
1 teaspoon instant coffee, dissolved in 1 teaspoon water
¼ teaspoon powdered cloves
4 egg whites, stiffly beaten
1 cup heavy cream, whipped until stiff
5 cups boiling water, for steaming

Bring water to boil in 6-quart pot tall enough to hold 1-quart tubed pudding form and its lid. Meanwhile, oil form and sprinkle inside with 2 teaspoons sugar. Grate nuts in blender at medium speed, a handful at a time, or use food mill. Beat ⅔ cup sugar and egg yolks together until lemon colored and forming bubbles; add chocolate, dissolved coffee, and cloves. Add grated nuts and stir well. Add one-quarter of beaten egg whites and stir, then fold in rest of egg whites. Pour batter into oiled and sugar-sprinkled pudding form, cover, and lock lid. Place in center of 6-quart pot with water for steaming, cover, return to boil, reduce heat, and steam for 15 minutes. Place in fireless cooker for 3 to 4 hours. At serving time, loosen edges of the cake from walls and tube with pointed knife and turn upside down to unmold. Cake will not have crust; if you want crust, place cake in 425° oven for 5 minutes. Serve hot or cold with whipped cream. Serves 6.

Making Yoghurt

Yoghurt-making in the fireless cooker is easy and inexpensive. Our friends Pumita and Avinash taught us this fireless-cooker method, which they learned in South Africa, and presto! we are now making excellent mild yoghurt and what we call "yocheese," which is like cream cheese.

The theory of yoghurt-making is simple: kill the bacteria in the milk to be used (remember Pasteur?) by scalding it at 180°, introduce live yeast bacteria from your "starter" when the temperature is down to 115°, and let the live bacteria go to work while the temperature falls slowly (4 to 5 hours). Then refrigerate the yoghurt right away.

If you have a thermometer measuring 115 to 180°, use it at least the first few times; later, trust your eyes and fingers.

Pour 1 quart of low-fat milk into a clean pot and heat it slowly, until the thermometer registers 180°F. or—an equally reliable gauge—until a skin forms on the surface of the milk. Remove the pan from the heating unit, remove the skin from the top, and let the milk cool to about 115°. Lacking a thermometer, test with your finger. If the milk seems just a little too hot for comfort, you are in the right temperature range.

For a starter, you need fresh yoghurt from a friend or from a store that carries a brand of live yoghurt (Continental, for example). Mix 1 to 2 tablespoons of starter per quart of milk with 2 tablespoons of heated milk. Add this mixture to the milk in the pot, or transfer all of it to a convenient container (a 1-quart mayonnaise jar works perfectly).* Distribute the starter evenly, cover, and pop it into your fireless cooker. After 5 hours take it out and check to see if it is firm. Refrigerate for 2 hours, and you have 1 quart of fresh, delicious yoghurt.

If you make a new batch of yoghurt within the next few days, you can use some of your own yoghurt as the starter. Or freeze the yoghurt in ice-cube trays and then use a cube of this for starter after it has thawed.

If you like your yoghurt especially firm, mix the starter with powdered milk. Experiment with more or less powdered milk to get the firmness you like.

To make yocheese, pour some of the yoghurt into a fine sieve or cheesecloth and let it drip for several hours or overnight. The whey will drip out and you will have a mild, delicious cheese that can be used as is or mixed with condiments for a spread.

*To make yoghurt-making even simpler, heat the milk directly in the jar in which the yoghurt will be stored. Put the jar containing the milk into a kettle containing 2 to 3 inches of water, which is kept boiling until the temperature of the milk reaches 180°. Remove the jar and let it cool until the temperature reaches 115°. Add the starter, cover, and put the jar into the cooker for 4 to 5 hours, then refrigerate. This method lets you avoid the tiresome task of scrubbing from the bottom of the pot the slight scorch that almost invariably forms when you heat milk directly in a pot.

Trouble Shooting

Problem: Distraction during the simmering. You don't know if the food has simmered too much or too little.

Solution: Don't worry! Put it into your fireless cooker. If the simmering time was too long, the food is likely to be only mildly overdone (unless, of course, you forgot it for hours). If the simmering time was too short, usually just a few extra minutes of cooking over direct heat before serving will correct the error.

Problem: You are late getting started with dinner preparations and there is not enough cooker time left.

Solution: Increase the simmering time slightly (for instance, 7 to 8 minutes for potatoes instead of the usual 5; 30 to 40 minutes for meat instead of the usual 20 to 30).

Problem: The potatoes are different sizes.

Solution: Choose reasonably equal medium-size potatoes for cooking in their jackets. They will usually all be done just right. If an extra-big one gets in by mistake and isn't quite done, no harm. Just take all the others out and boil the big one on the stove until it's done, usually not more than 5 to 7 minutes. If your potatoes are very large, use a recipe for which the potatoes will be peeled and quartered, but remember, the simmering time for quartered potatoes will be much shorter (1 to 2 minutes). You might also dice them for potato soup, or cook them peeled and quartered to be mashed just before serving.

Problem: Underdone food. It's serving time and you find your food underdone or cold.

Solution: Something went wrong with (a) your cooker, (b) your pot, or (c) your procedure.

a. If you have just made your cooker, it's possible that your container has a large gap or crack somewhere, the pillow is too small for adequate tuck-in, the cooker's lid doesn't fit properly, the pillow is so fat that the lid cannot be closed, or you stuffed the cooker unevenly, perhaps leaving a large air pocket. Or the pot is too tall for the nest in your cooker so that the pot rises above the stuffing and the pillow cannot be tucked around the pot to make a tight fit.

Solution: Simmer the food on your stove until done, usually only 5 to 10 minutes. Your hungry family may growl but the food should be perfectly all right—with dinner only a little late.

b. Something went wrong with your pot. Steam escaped somehow between pot and lid. Perhaps the lid is bent or is the wrong lid for the pot or got jiggled during transfer. Perhaps you chose the wrong pot for the amount of food you are cooking.

Solution: Finish the cooking on the stove. Take comfort in the fact that you're still using much less time and fuel than you would with ordinary cooking methods.

c. Something went wrong with your procedure. You looked up a recipe for green beans but you are cooking dry beans, or you used instructions for peeled and quartered potatoes, but you are boiling them in their jackets.

Solution: Complete the cooking right then, if a few minutes will do it. If the food is badly underdone, as in the case of dried beans, look up the correct recipe, give the pot adequate simmering time, and return it to the cooker. (You may have to stoop so low as to open a can of beans to feed your family.)

Another procedural problem: You forgot to put on the top pillow or you put it on hastily, allowing heat to leak. Or a corner of your pillow got caught under the lid and it didn't close properly. Perhaps you forgot to close the lid.

Solution: Complete cooking on the stove.

Problem: Overcooked vegetables. All the vegetables in your stew look limp and discolored and taste blah.

Solution: Either your simmering time or your cooker time (or both) may be too long for these particular vegetables. You can't rescue this batch but next time try cooking your meat alone as suggested in the recipe; then take the pot out of your cooker about an hour before serving time, add the vegetables, bring to a boil, simmer for 5 minutes, and return to the cooker. However, very tender fresh vegetables may get overdone even with this procedure—you will soon be able to tell ahead of time which ones (for example, greens like beet tops or very young green beans). You can add them just a few minutes before serving and complete the stew by cooking very briefly on the stove. Sometimes overcooked vegetables can be salvaged for soups. Overdone potatoes often taste fine when mashed.

UNDER DONE

OVER DONE

153

Problem: Underdone meat. Everything was done as the recipe advised, but the pot roast didn't get done.

Solution: If you used frozen meat, perhaps you did not thaw it completely before you started to cook it. Careful thawing is important for all methods of preparing frozen foods and roasts, but particularly when preparing them for the fireless cooker. If meat is still frozen on the inside, it is possible for the water in the pot to boil quite actively so that you *think* you can start your simmering time, but the meat will be far from heated through. Therefore, *be sure all meat is thoroughly thawed* before you start cooking it.

Perhaps the meat was a very tough cut. If it's mildly underdone, complete the cooking on the stove. Or repeat the simmering time and return the pot to the fireless cooker. If the meat is badly underdone, it may need up to 2 more hours in the cooker.

The roast may have been very thick—more than 2 or 3 inches. In this case, cut it into 2 or 3 pieces and proceed as in preceding paragraph.

Problem: A rarely used fireless cooker. Your initial enthusiasm for the fireless cooker has tapered off. You find yourself forgetting to plan to use it or you use it only for a few basic recipes.

Solution: Remind yourself why you wanted a fireless cooker. Read the section on adapting your own favorite recipes for the fireless cooker (page 34) and reread the section on its advantages (page 8).

Planning Fireless-Cooker Meals

FOR A FAMILY OR CROWD

Instead of requiring a more or less hectic half-hour to an hour before dinner for meal preparation, the fireless cooker requires time—often very little—for preparation earlier in the day. I would suggest that for your first fireless-cooker dish you start

1 to 2 hours before serving time, choose something requiring a short cooker time (rice or potatoes), and make leisurely preparations—say on a weekend. Later, when you are familiar with quite a few recipes and confident that your new kitchen tool works well, use recipes with longer cooker periods, planning to do the simmering in the morning.

Morning, I realize, is a busy time in many households, but I have learned to find a few minutes for simmering something simple in order to get it into the cooker. This saves much more time later when I come home tired and hungry to face other demands on my time and attention.

Another good idea, if possible, is to plan dinner for one to two hours after you come home. Do the simmering right after you get home and put the food into the cooker. Then you have time to relax, read, or if everyone is very hungry, have a snack or appetizer.

No active family gets by without the occasional "crazy day": work, school, music, ballgame, dinner guests, dentist, a lost pet or other mix-ups. For such a day, a good plan is for the first person home (from teen-ager to grandfather) to simmer something simple and put it into the cooker.

For informal entertaining, the one-dish recipes are good. They can be prepared earlier in the day and need only a few minutes for finishing touches at serving time. For a crowd or for an occasional fancy party, the fireless cooker will make things easier by allowing you to make the more involved items one or more hours before serving, then have them out of the way in the cooker, hot and ready when needed.

If you are planning a long, hard day that will take you away from home for many hours, but you are reluctant to get involved with lengthy meal preparations in the morning, let me suggest that you cook legumes. The night before, soak the food—for instance beans—right in the pot in which you intend to cook it. In the morning, put this pot on the stove for the 15-minute simmering time while you prepare for work or eat breakfast, and put the pot into the cooker before you leave. When you come home it should take only a few minutes to add last-minute touches like seasoning, thickening, vegetables, or already-cooked meat (maybe ham or sausage).

When using meat for boiling or for stew, a similar two-step plan can be used. For such dishes, put on a large pot with water first thing when you get to the kitchen in the morning. When it comes to a boil, add the meat and let it simmer for the required simmering time of 20 to 30 minutes while you do other morning chores, then put it into the cooker before you leave for work. In the evening when you get home, bring the meat to a full rolling boil again, add whatever vegetables you plan to use about 15 to 20 minutes before you intend to serve, season, and let it all simmer on the stove until done. For this situation, you could plan to have potatoes, noodles, or a similar food already cooked and in the refrigerator; you need only to fry or heat it.

Remember to boil all foods containing meat for several minutes before serving whenever your cooker time is more than 4 hours.

If you or someone else in the family has enough energy left at this time of day to put together the ingredients for a steamed pudding, it can go into the cooker at the time you take the main course out and, since the cooker times for these desserts are very short, it will be done in time for dessert or perhaps for after-dinner guests.

"CAN JOHNNIE STAY FOR DINNER?"

A special type of entertaining occurs when children invite their friends for a meal. When our children were young, one or occasionally all four of them would bring home a friend for a meal almost every day. The fireless cooker made it possible to let them eat with us without much extra cost or work. The foods that lend themselves to fireless cooking, like soups or stews, can be stretched to feed extra diners. They also fit the general policy of avoiding waste. Family and friends all can be easily served family style, everyone helping himself to as much or as little as he wants and feeling free to eat more of one food and less of another: free to try anything new and leave it on the plate if he doesn't like it.

All this was entirely new to our children's friends. They came from homes where rules about table manners were strict: eat at least some of every food served, and eat all food on your plate—the food invariably being dished up by someone with more appetite than the youngster had. Of course, if the plate was not cleaned there was no dessert. These rules can lead to overeating or to other feeding problems, but persist for the convenience of the cook and are promoted by food packaged in units.

If we had used these rules, the friends of our children would never have enjoyed eating at our house. Most of the food served was new to them but, because they were entirely free to choose, they could experiment and eventually learn to like most of what we served, as did our own children. No one ever had to eat the occasionally disliked food or to finish anything, yet waste was rare. Dessert was never junk food, but was part of a well-balanced diet and therefore never withheld. And if there was not very much of it—as in the case of the first strawberries of the season—it became a lesson in sharing.

Incidentally, this approach makes mealtime more enjoyable for the adults in the family, too, because they're not spending it battling with the children.

USING LEFTOVERS

The words *leftovers* and *remnants* create a bad image in the minds of many. This is unfortunate because some of the most inspired dishes have their origin in the need to use good food left over from another meal. Nowadays, families are getting smaller, yet most food is packaged in units that no longer fit family needs.

A whole chicken is too much for only my husband and me. If the butcher cuts and separates it into parts it gets even more expensive, and if I buy packaged chicken parts, I am forced to buy too much. Therefore, I use the fireless cooker to help me plan chicken for more than one meal.

Any of hundreds of good recipes can be used for this first cooking, whether I roast, boil, broil, or whatever. (I always cook the giblets at the same time to make gravy or chicken stock.) What is "left over" after the first meal is really "planned over" to become an attractive meal in its own right.

The fireless cooker helps to make this kind of planning efficient, with long cooker times for large quantities, short cooker times for small quantities. The most efficient cooking happens in the fireless cooker during the first 4 to 5 hours. After this, the gradually dropping temperature serves mostly to keep the food warm —for another 3 to 4 hours if the quantity is 2 quarts or more.

FOR VEGETARIANS

Meat was served in my childhood home when it was available—perhaps three or four times weekly. So, as part of my experience with the fireless cooker, I remember many good vegetarian meals. A great favorite as a dinner was creamed spinach with fried eggs on top, fried polenta and carrots, and potato dumplings for dessert. The special appeal of this menu was at least partly in the attractive colors. Served with milk and bread and perhaps with fruit and cheese instead of the dumplings, this menu would be nutritionally excellent.

Because meal-balancing becomes particularly important in vegetarian cooking, some suggested dinner menus are given here. I should note that if I were doing the cooking, the meal would always include bread.

Potato Soup, Rice with Tomato Sauce, salad, and Cottage Cheese Pudding.

Dumplings with Mushroom Sauce, salad, and apricot cake.

Vegetable Soup, Potatoes in the Jacket, Creamed Cabbage, and Rice and Apple Pudding.

Potato Patties, mushroom soufflé, green salad, and prune whip.

Lentil Soup, hard-cooked eggs with salad (Potato Salad, Cauliflower Salad, or green salad), and fresh fruit with cream.

Minestrone, Dumpling in a Napkin, cucumber salad, and Cream of Wheat Pudding.

COOKING FOR SMALL HOUSEHOLDS

My good friend Dorothy, who lives alone, tells me that it is worthwhile for her to use her fireless cooker regularly but not daily. She uses only the 3-quart pot for which her cooker was made and mostly she prepares soups or stews in 2-quart quantities. Some of what is left after the first meal is refrigerated for a second meal within the same week. The rest, to be frozen, she ladles into a few 1-pound cottage-cheese containers, because she has found that these are just the right size for a meal for one. She has also found that it's better not to use potatoes in her stews or soups because they don't freeze well. When the time comes for thawing and reheating, it takes only about 7 minutes to cook peeled potatoes (cut into 1-by-2-inch cubes) with the rest of the stew.

Rice and noodles, which also don't freeze well, are best cooked separately, noodles on the stove just before serving and rice in the fireless cooker in a 1½-quart pot. Rice leftovers are easy to use up fried or in the next day's soup, pudding, soufflé, or casserole.

Following are some pointers and adaptations of fireless-cooker recipes for one- or two-person households.

Potatoes: Potatoes can be cooked in quantity with two or three meals in mind. But if the cook wants to cook potatoes for just one meal, this can be done, too. Use any pot that fits the cooker, simply adding enough water, as always, so that the pot is two-thirds full.

Root vegetables: The same method can be used with carrots, beets, or turnips for just one serving, as for potatoes.

Use a 5-minute simmer time and a 1-hour minimum cooker time. (In this case, however, be sure to save the water because peeled and cut vegetables will lose a considerable amount of nutritionally valuable substances to the cooking water.) Still, it's easier—and saves time and energy—to plan these vegetables for at least two meals. With beets, for instance, you might make Borscht for the first meal, dice some beets for Harvard Beets for the second meal, and slice the remainder to serve cold with a Vinaigrette Dressing for the third meal.

Boiled beef: This is a recipe that can be readily cut in half or even less. Use the smallest practical pot and fill it two-thirds full with the beef, vegetables, and water. Here no nutritional value is lost since the broth is either served with this meal or another. Leftover beef can be eaten cold on sandwiches, warmed in Brown Gravy, or served as a delicious salad diced with a sour-cream dressing or any other dressing.

Steamed puddings and soufflés: The 3- or 4-quart pot can be used with 1 quart of water to steam foods as for the regular recipes in Steamed Foods, but a smaller pudding mold should be used. Cut ingredient amounts in half and prepare as usual. If no small pudding mold with a good lid is available, tin cans can be substituted, topped with foil, and tied. Several such cans can be prepared in a larger pot at the same time and refrigerated or frozen for later use.

Dumplings: Dumpling in a Napkin lends itself to preparation in a small quantity. Cut the recipe in half or less and prepare it in the fireless cooker in a small pot, remembering the general rule that the pot must be two-thirds full. But I consider it so particularly good fried the next day, with or without a beaten egg stirred over it, or served with Brown Gravy or Mushroom Sauce, that I always make the full recipe to be sure I have some left over. All dumpling recipes can be adjusted for smaller quantities.

When small quantities are to be cooked in the fireless cooker, it is well to remember that small pots will stay hot enough and cook the food adequately so long as cooker times are short (1 to 1½ hours). You may want to experiment.

FOR THE COOK WITH A HANDICAP

If a person enjoys cooking, and the independence of cooking for oneself, but suffers from an impairment of one hand, I suggest using a fireless cooker that is placed at a convenient height close to the stove and is either in a drawer or equipped with a lid that can be opened and closed easily with one hand. The fireless cooker should have a mechanism that holds the lid open securely while the cook is taking out and putting in a pot. It is important to have single-handled 2- to 3-quart pots; the handles should be short—not more than 3 inches—and the pots should be lightweight; stainless steel is excellent. With a few special kitchen tools for one-handed operation, or perhaps with a blender or food processor, it should be possible to make many of the recipes in this book.

I hope that people with other handicaps, including people confined to wheelchairs, will enjoy the convenience and other advantages of the fireless cooker. If the handicap, chronic illness, or old age is so incapacitating that cooking for oneself is not possible, I believe that the fireless cooker can still help by making in-home care easier. If a family member, friend, or neighbor can cook a meal for an invalid conveniently at the same time as cooking for his or her own family (by placing part

of the meal in a portable cooker to be delivered later), a lot of the work and annoyance can be taken out of this kind of service and the patient will enjoy home-cooked meals.

Meals on Wheels–type programs could be improved by use of fireless cookers. The food would cook its normal time during transport, arriving fresh and tasty rather than acquiring the institutional taste that comes, mainly, from being kept warm too long.

Other Uses for the Cooker

Keeping food warm until serving time. If you take a roast out of the oven to "rest" before carving, make the gravy, and find that either the rest of the dinner or your hungry crowd is not ready, it's great to be able to pop the gravy into the cooker to stay warm. The same is true of vegetables that do best with short cooking periods: green peas, young spinach, or zucchini. Unless you really can leave the cooking of these foods for the last minute, you will find them overcooking, being in the way, needing supervision, or getting cold. In the cooker they will be okay.

Keeping food warm for second helpings. This is particularly easy if the food was cooked in the fireless cooker. Serve the food directly from the pot, still in the cooker, and then close the lid promptly, putting the pillow back. The food will easily stay warm up to 45 minutes. If you take the pot out, serve everyone at the table, and then take the pot back to the cooker, it will still stay warm for 20 to 30 minutes, depending on the size of the pot and how long it was out. If you have a crowd to serve, the food is likely to cool off considerably. In this case, to keep it warm 45 minutes or longer, bring the food to the boiling point briefly, cover it, and then put it into the cooker.

Solving the problem of different eating schedules. Dinner can be served for one group of people, returned to the heating unit, brought to the boiling point briefly, and placed back in the cooker. It will be hot, delicious, and not overcooked 2 or 3 hours later when the next group of people arrives for dinner.

But I don't recommend more than one reboil and back-to-cooker procedure, because with several simmering periods, overcooking takes place and the results are disappointing.

Keeping food hot over steam. Certain foods don't lend themselves to reboiling or reheating—for instance, rice or noodles—but the fireless cooker can keep this type of food attractive and tasty. Use a covered pot large enough to accommodate a folding steamer (see sketch) in which you have placed your food for reheating. Put about 2 cups of water into the bottom of the pot, put the steamer into the pot, and cover. Bring to boil and place in the cooker. The food will be hot and attractive up to 2 hours later.

Doubling as a cooler. Because a fireless cooker is simply a device to keep food well insulated, it serves as well to keep food or beverages cold as it does to keep them warm.

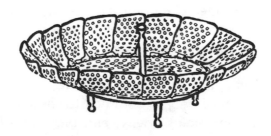

A quart of ice cream can be surrounded with ice cubes in a large pot and put into the cooker. A brick of blue ice (sold commercially in grocery stores or sporting-goods shops) placed on top of milk or drinks within the nest of the cooker will keep them cold for many hours. Avoid trying to package ice from your own freezer —dripping is almost inevitable. For short periods—an hour or two—food will stay cold without ice in the cooker.

A portable fireless cooker taken on a picnic or camping trip can do double duty, serving both as a cooler and as a cooker.

Supplementing a one-heating-unit kitchen. When our youngest son Tim was in college, he beat the cost of living by buying an ancient Navy truck for very little money. He built himself a bed, shelves, and a miniature kitchen from scrap lumber and acquired a single heating unit and enough stray kitchen utensils to do his own cooking. When he came home that year for Christmas, he asked me to make him the smallest possible fireless cooker, knowing that I would be delighted to tackle such a job. The cooker I built was 12 inches high and 14 by 14 inches across and was furnished with four pillows filled with styrofoam pellets. Since the old truck, when in motion, rocked like a small boat on the high seas, the cooker was bolted securely in place on the floor under the tiny kitchen table.

He went on long trips in the old truck, sometimes with one or two friends, crossing most of the continent while commuting between college, home, and work. He would cook one mainstay meal, such as potatoes or rice, for the required simmering time on the single burner, then put the pot into the fireless cooker. At serving time he used the single unit for frying meat or sausage. I suppose if there was to be a vegetable or some other cooked item it had to be kept warm in the bed. But in any case, he liked the arrangement. Students or others with minimal cooking set-ups may find a small or portable fireless cooker helpful if only one heating unit is available.

The fireless cooker in these circumstances can serve instead of an oven for recipes that use the cooker as a steamer (see Steamed Foods).

Cooking on camping trips. Our eldest son Chris has used the principle of fireless cooking on camping trips. He usually cooks for groups of seven or more, using either a campfire or a Coleman-type stove. He tells me that a fireless cooker is handy when the car brings all the equipment to the campsite. In this situation a meal is prepared at home, just before departure, in the usual way. Then, just before placing the pot in the fireless cooker, Chris likes to tape the lid to the pot to avoid steam loss and spillage. On arrival at the campsite, the meal is ready to be eaten, and later the cooker is useful for keeping foods hot or cold.

Cooking while backpacking. For mountain trips or backpacking, even a lightweight portable cooker would be a cumbersome extra, so, for many years of mountaineering, Chris has used instead the principle of fireless cooking, substituting a sleeping bag as a fireless cooker.

Of course pots get black on the bottom and sides when used over an open campfire and, although to a lesser degree, on a Coleman stove. Therefore Chris uses foil or large sheets of heavy plastic around the pots before tucking them into a sleeping bag. The same wrapping is used to protect other camping gear from soot when equipment is being carried between campsites.

For trips to the high mountains Chris uses precooked dried foods. These require very little cooking and would not normally go into a cooker, but since they're cooked one at a time, Chris can put them into the sleeping bag to stay warm until an entire meal is ready. But he uses the sleeping bag for more than keeping food warm, and has found it particularly useful as a fireless cooker for rice or other grains. These foods, when cooked over a campfire, burn easily or stick to the pan, making a problem at clean-up time, but they do not stick and require only short cooker periods when wrapped in his sleeping bag. Recipes using longer cooker times, like beans, are useful on trips if the camper is returning to the same site at the end of a day's hiking.

Bibliography

Cather, Willa Sibert. *My Antonia.* Cambridge: Riverside Press, 1918.
This novel about small-town life in the Midwest at the turn of the century revolves around a family that had recently immigrated to the U.S. from Bohemia. The fireless cooker is mentioned as part of the family's kitchen equipment.

Curtis, Isabel Gordon. *Mrs. Curtis's Cookbook.* New York: The Success Company, 1909.
This book is at the back of, and bound with, another book by a different author: Morse, Sidney L., *Household Discoveries.* New York: The Success Company, 1908. Subtitled *Encyclopedia of Practical Recipes and Processes,* the Curtis book contains seven pages of instructions for making and using a fireless cooker, plus seven recipes and timetables giving stove-top simmering times and cooker times for many different types of foods. The time-tables seem badly out of step with current ideas about cooking, but all the other information is still pertinent.

Editors of *Organic Gardening Magazine. Build it Better Yourself.* Emmaus, Pennsylvania: Rodale Press, 1977.
Gives instructions for making a fireless cooker, which the editors call a Hot Box. They describe two methods of construction, both accommodating only one size pot, and give very short, rather confusing instructions on its use.

Lenz, Sigfried. *The German Lesson.* Hamburg: Hoffman & Kempe, 1968.
The fireless cooker is mentioned as standard kitchen equipment in this novel about a family in a small town in Schleswig-Hostein, Northern Germany, during World War II.

Mayor Mitchell's Food Supply Committee. *Hints to Housewives.* New York City: 1917.

Contains five pages on making and using a fireless cooker with a few representative recipes. This came to my attention through two articles that appeared in the Seattle *Post-Intelligencer* on October 8 and October 15, 1975. The articles quoted the pamphlet, gave instructions for making and using a fireless cooker, and quoted some of the recipes.

Women for Peace. *Wonder Cooking and Simply Living.* South Africa: city and date not available.

The editors' logo shows the profiles of three women representing the three racial groups of South Africa: black, "colored," and white, suggesting equality and cooperation. The pamphlet contains nutritional information, good instructions for making and using a fireless cooker, and several recipes geared to the needs of rural black families in South Africa. Two of the recipes—Steamed Whole Wheat Bread and Boston Steamed Brown Bread—were adapted to Western cooking terms for this book.

Index